Making the World Go Away

Thriving in End-times & Beyond

Making the World Go Away

Thriving in End-times & Beyond

Ruth L. Miller

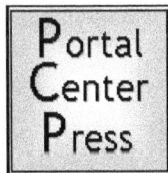

Portal
Center
Press

Making the World Go Away: Thriving in end-times & beyond.
Updated and expanded 3rd edition ©2021 Ruth L. Miller

2nd edition title: *Making the World Go Away: A Babyboomer's guide to end-times* © 2018 Ruth L. Miller

Original edition title: *Make the World Go Away: the gift of 2012* © 2010; 2013 (ISBN: 978-1-936902-00-2)

ISBN: 978-1-936902-27-9
Portal Center Press
Oregon

Printed in USA

Contents

Introduction

People in our culture are fascinated with end-times. For a thousand years many Europeans, and now Americans, have anticipated the end of the world with a mixture of terror and delight; hope and despair. And nowadays that fascination is reaching new heights, with good reason: many things are changing around us and humanity really wants to be living in a different kind of world!

This book was originally written in 2010, after I had been asked numerous times to explain what was going on then. With so many people focused on "end times," "earth changes," and 2012, and so many books out there telling us that the forecasts and prophecies all pointed to something big happening on or about the winter solstice of that year, it was easy to get caught up in the hype and rhetoric. Most of us found we must choose one line of reasoning and accept it or get lost in the confusion of messages.

The one essential question was then, and still, with so many people so concerned about catastrophic earth changes or the Second Coming, really is: "What's the world coming to?"

For years as a professional futurist my job was to forecast emerging possibilities and probable developments based on current trends and potential surprises. The groups I worked with studied how people made decisions and we developed methods that would encourage more effective decisions about long-range possibilities. We predicted the impacts of policies and technologies and helped governments and organizations figure out how to accomplish their goals in the face of changing economies and sociopolitical norms.

That research says that something's got to give, and soon. As we hear every day, the way we are living is using up resources and damaging the earth's capacity to replace and recharge, far faster than we can undo the damage. Much of the data we collected and many of the computer models we ran told us that most heavily-used energy resources, food production capacity, and clean water would drop far below the world population's needs between 2010 and 2040. Geophysicists and astronomers tell us that solar activity, combined with shifting climate patterns, will cause significant damage to coastal areas by 2030 – a pattern that is already well underway. The interconnected web of finance and industry is stretched almost to its limits and, as the "Great Recession" of 2008 demonstrated, is precariously on the edge of collapse. The desperation of oppressed migrants, the rising inequality in so-called democracies, and a cascade of mental disorders, including dementia, post-traumatic stress, mass murder and suicide – are all indicators of societal breakdown.

Clearly, major shifts are underway, and many peoples' lives are being severely disrupted, since the fate of individuals is inexo-rably tied to the breakdown of their social norms. That has always been true, but now, with growing populations, climate change, and shrinking resources, the system is so distressed that human extinc-tion has become a real possibility.

Yet the research also shows that all those systems, and hu-manity as a whole, are far more resilient than we tend to think, and that what appears to be a disaster in one moment can actually have far less negative long-term and remote consequences than we used to fear. In short, the breakdown may not be so bad, after all.

So should we pay attention to all those announcements of "end times?"

Yes, because something is indeed ending. No, if "paying at-tention" means acting out of fear. This is no time to panic.

There are two different approaches to understanding the change we're in. One uses calendars and charts to describe longterm patterns and cycles; the other looks for signs and por-tents. Both of them are saying that the way of life we've become used to is ending.

The calendar approach is based on calculations of star posi-tions, like the Mayan "Great Cycle" chart. It says that the winter solstice of 2012 was the beginning of the end of a 5,125-year period that is the last phase of a larger cycle (which westerners call "precession", which relates to the changing position of the sunrise relative to the center of the Milky Way galaxy, and December 12, 2021 was the end of that period. The ancient Hindu scriptures, the Vedas, call the larger cycles, which last about 26,000 years, *yugas*, and say that each one has its own characteristics – this past yuga being characterized by chaos and violence and increasing use (and abuse) of power; it ended February 11, 2021. The Chinese, using the hexagrams of the *I Ching*, or Book of Changes, and Chinese astronomical and astrological traditions, say that this same period completes the cycle of changes represented by those hexagrams, the most recent ending with the lunar new year of 2020. Modern social historians like Alastair Taylor and Pitirim Sorokin suggest that the rise and fall of cultures have predictable patterns that repeat themselves. All of the above say that at this time, right now, one era with certain qualities is ending, while another, with very different qualities, is beginning.

The second approach is prevalent among ancient, indigenous peoples and is tied to signs and portents. In North America, for example, "when the eagle lands on the moon" has long been prophesied as the turning point for native peoples in relation to the U.S. government. And, within days of Neil Armstrong's July, 1969, announcement that "The Eagle has landed," the first bill permitting Native American to engage in their traditional spiritual practices on reservation lands was introduced into Congress. For some, the determination of Caucasian children to discover and practice native ways is another sign. For most indigenous peoples, this age, or "world," is one of several that humanity has experienced, and we are on the brink of ending one and beginning another. For all, the near-extinction of native elders and the recent revival of native ways is one of the most important signs that this past cycle or "world" is nearly over. Another is the creation of the "gourd of ashes" (what the Hopi call the atomic or nuclear bomb) which, when dropped, boils everything away and makes it impossible for anything to grow for a years, is, for Hopi elders, the sign that this ending will not be peaceful and easy.

The Christian concept of the Second Coming is based on the signs described in the apocalyptic vision ("apocalypse" coming from a Greek term meaning "lifting the veil") described by John in the final book, "The Revelation," of the New Testament. In that work an exile tells of hearing a voice and falling onto his back, then seeing a vision of a war between Good and Evil played out in the skies above. In his vision, millions of people die from illness, famine, earth changes, and warfare, all over the world. Some scholars see John's Revelation as a forecast of Rome's end and the beginning of a new, Christian era. Others, especially fundamentalist Christians, link these images with apocalyptic lines from the Old Testament and Gospels, creating a powerful prophetic vision for humanity that many see becoming manifest in today's world.

The Muslim tradition, drawing on many of the same sources, with additions from the *Q'uran* and other writings, offers yet another vision of one world ending and another beginning – with many signs and indicators showing up in today's news.

All the prophecies and forecasts tell us, then, that now, these first decades of the 21st century, are years of change for humanity – and may be a period of transformation into a way of life that is very different.

That we should be paying attention to – and even celebrate!

What do they say? What possibilities can we expect?

There's not a whole lot of agreement among the prophets and the forecasters, but one thing is clear – at this point a lot of people are going to be leaving one way of life and beginning another, radically different, way of living.

The Mayans are the most explicit about what the "new world" will be. The bits and pieces that have been gleaned from a few remaining books, called *codices*, and story-pillars, called *stelae*, tell us that we're moving into a time when people are less interested in mechanical or electrical devices and more interested in biological and spiritual development. They suggest that the sociocultural pendulum will inevitably be swinging back: away from empire-building toward community-building, away from rocket science toward spiritual science, and away from computers toward consciousness.

Prophecies from the North American native cultures say that, if the transformation is violent, only the "children of the earth" will survive, living in the mountains and forests, away from urban centers. If it is peaceful, then the native elders will be able to teach large numbers of people of all colors how to live in harmony with each other, with the Creator's teachings, and with the Earth.

The Christian prophecies, drawn from a combination of biblical sources, including the books of Revelation, Isaiah, Jeremiah, and Daniel, along with a little Matthew and Paul and interpretations from Protestant and Catholic mystics, say we'll see a thousand years of violent shifts and changes, culminating in "a new heaven and a new earth' in a crystal "new Jerusalem" with the "river of life" flowing from the roots of the "Tree of Life" at its center. Some folks say we're completing that thousand years of violence, now.

Recently, independent prophecies, mostly from apprentice shamans and self-proclaimed "channels" of "higher wisdom" suggest that we'll either be barely surviving in a world whose geography has totally changed, or we'll be developing ever-stronger psychic and spiritual abilities in small, interconnected communities around the globe.[1] Earlier prophecies by Edgar Cayce and Ruth Montgomery include elements of both.

Futurists, also, are divided, as they have been all along.

Some futurists are committed to the "official forecasts." They project a world where massive alternative energy facilities and carefully monitored banking systems continue to support the development of new technologies so that up to 12 billion people can live relatively comfortable, urban and suburban lives with computers and the internet replacing TVs and radio. They see food being produced hydroponically in homes and warehouses, global and interplanetary commerce and travel being the norm, and the health-care industry finding ever-more-miraculous tools and ap-

---

[1] Some resources for these include books by Mary Summer Rain, "Ramtha," Ken Carey, and the *Bringers of the Dawn* series.

proaches to address physical disease and injury. Some of them
continue to center all these developments in northern Europe and
the U.S., but more and more envision the centers of innovation
and commerce moving into Asia and India.[2]

Some futurists are committed to the "breakdown forecasts."
They project a world where either a catastrophe or the steady de-
pletion of resources, including energy, soil, and clean water, lead
to increasing violence and disruption of political systems so that
the infrastructure necessary for an industrial culture decays or is
destroyed and more and more people would be left without work
and without resources for survival, leading to more violence, and
ultimately a feudalistic "war lord" society, not unlike the worst of
China's or Europe's "dark ages," or parts of the Middle East or
Africa, today. Robert Heinlein's novel *Friday* depicts this scenario
pretty clearly, and his *Revolt in 2100* takes it even further for the
U.S.

Very few futurists project the kind of changes that the prophecies predict – simply because the specifics of the prophecies have
not yet fit the numbers futurists have been tracking or the algo-
rithms used by their computer programs. But those who do are
hopeful. Scenarios ranging from "The Apocalyptic Transformation"[3] to what can only be called "Heaven on Earth,"[4] are
based on a major shift in thought processes among a vast majority
of the world's population, leading to a new world culture based,
not on violence or competition, but on cooperative development
of resources using appropriate technology to maximize long-term
returns, dynamic stability, and optimal productivity. Among these
scenarios, the end result is the same peaceful, harmonious life that
is suggested in the prophecies; only the means by which we get
there varies.

---

[2] Most of the material published by and presented at meetings of The
World Future Society is along these lines.
[3] This scenario was first published in a research report directed by Duane
Elgin in 1975 by the Center for the Study of Social Policy at Stanford Research Institute, and then expanded in 1980 in a book called *Seven
Tomorrows* by Peter Schwartz, Paul Hawken, and Jay Ogilvie.
[4] Duane Elgin's *Awakening Earth* is a prime example.

But which of these is really going to happen?

All of them. That's really why I stopped being a professional futurist. After almost 20 years of "crunching numbers" and following trends, I realized that each and every scenario we worked out was happening somewhere now, or would be soon. The "breakdown" forecasts are happening on several continents and in the decaying urban cores and desertified mining regions of the U.S. The "official" forecasts are happening in the new cities of China, the Muslim countries, Germany, and in some areas of almost every industrialized country. The "transformation" scenarios are emerging in ever-greater numbers in small hill-country and coastal communities all around the world. The Great Shift described in these scenarios won't happen everywhere, all at once, but is unfolding gradually, here and there, as small populations transform a culture to reflect their change in consciousness from one of scarcity to one of abundance, from growth to sustainability, and from domination to cooperation.

What does that mean - all of them are going to happen? How do we work with that?

It's actually wonderful that they're all happening somewhere now. It means we get to choose what future we want to live, and we can do so by choosing where and how we live, today!

If we want a high-tech, polished sky-scraper, urban future, we can move to where that's happening, give up whatever doesn't fit, and adapt ourselves to that kind of environment. If we want a "cowboy," "G-I Joe," "Paladin," or "gang-fight" future, we can go where that's happening and do likewise. And if we want to live in a world where people work together to create a life in harmony with natural processes and spiritual guidance, we can do that, too.

In fact, different ways of being on the planet will make it possible for more people to have different kinds of resources longer than if we all lived the same way – at least for the short term. It turns out that these different ways of living, these sub-cultures, can be sustained only as long as there are people and resources and spaces for them to continue. That may be a few years or a few generations, depending on how well each group conserves resources or are effective in finding new ones. The current interest in Mars and the asteroids is part of one group's effort to maintain a hi-tech future for as long as possible.

However, if, as some people are suggesting, a solar flare were to burn out a substantial number of electronic devices, it may be possible to sustain the "official, hi-tech" future for only a few people in a relatively small area. If, as the computer models suggest, lack of resources for large-scale agriculture makes it impossible to ship food into some urban cores, those people will have to find new ways to produce food, or move out if they are to survive. As they do so, they'll leave behind blocks and blocks of empty buildings for scavengers to live off of – until weather, fire, and decomposition wear them down to ruins. If hungry, angry, fearful urban gangs decide to take over the lands and food supplies of nearby cooperative harmonious communities, then those communities' quality of life will be greatly reduced, too – and the non-farming gangs who stole the land and food supply will slowly die because they don't know how to produce what they need.[5]

What can we do about it, so late in the process?

It would have been nice if we'd paid attention back in the 1970s and '80s, when all the forecasts and prophecies began to tell us these changes were coming. We could have implemented policies then to ease the shift we're headed into, or simply kept in place policies like the ones that the Carter administration introduced to help reduce the impacts.

It's not useful now, though, to look back and see all the ways we could have done something different once. It's far more useful to use the tools and resources that have emerged in the interim to create what might possibly get us through this process and to the other side – into the new era or "world" that is emerging, now.

---

[5] Several "post-apocalyptic" books and movies have illustrated this. In the 1960s, there were the books *Alas, Babylon,* and *A Canticle for Liebowitz,* and the film *What Have They Done to the Rain?* The 1980s gave us *Mad Max* and *A Dog and His Boy.* The 1990s brought Stephen King's *The Stand.* And, in the past decade, *Independence Day* and *2012* offer other visions.

For the long term – that is, beyond a couple generations – we need to focus on creating a way of life that is both sustainable and harmonious with our inner being, and begin to move in that direction. We need to discover what we truly want from life and develop the skills and resources that allow us to experience that. We need to learn how to make the world we have been living in go away and begin to build a new one that will support a peaceful life for all. Then we can apply those skills and teach our children to do the same.

And that's what this book is about.

But it's not a "how-to" guide for an ecologically and politically sustainable culture, nor is it about the physical actions we must take. That's another book[6] and many useful resources can be found on the internet today. Instead, this book is about how we got to the point of being able to make such a choice and how our thoughts and words *can get us through and beyond it*. It's about the mental, emotional, and metaphysical processes – the ways and means beyond the physical – that can bring forth a truly sustainable culture, the "new heaven and new earth" that many of us are hoping cam emerge in our daily lives. It's about how each of us can live the life of freedom and mutual support that is our birthright: here, now, and for the foreseeable future, regardless of what the world around us seems to be going through. This is what the founders of the great democracies offered in past centuries, and what we are literally on the brink of, globally, today.

In these pages, we'll explore the way our thoughts and actions got us into this situation, and how they can get us through it. We'll look in detail at some of the prophecies for guidelines on the most effective strategies to use. And we'll look at the processes and practices that will help us dissolve a "world" that no longer works for most of us as we begin to create a new one that can let us all experience life, liberty, and fulfillment..

Blessings on the journey!

---

[6] *Thriving on Planet Earth: a future for humanity.* Ruth L. Miller, published by Portal Center Press.

Chapter 1: Make the World Go Away[7]

During the 1950-60s, when the Baby-boomer generation was growing up, the world was, for the first time, a sea of electronic signals, filled with song and politics. With transistor radios glued to our ears and "TV trays" replacing dining room tables, we learned how to sing and dance and understand how the world works by watching and listening to celebrity entertainers, commercials, and the news. Song lyrics defined our emotional state, and newscasters defined our world – which meant that what happened in the classroom or family became increasingly irrelevant with each passing hour.

According to those sources, the world was wonderful and getting better every day, and we believed it – until we watched Walter Cronkite cry on that fateful day we all remember, in November of 1963. That day the world fell apart. Camelot ended. The age of "ever-better" and "progress is our most important product" was over. And, in our hearts, we knew it. We were crying as much for the end of the dream as we were for the shock of our president's assassination.

So, even though officially the Baby-boomer generation began about 1942 and ended in 1962, psychologically, a generation is defined by shared memories and the values that go with them. And Baby-boomers don't remember World War II or VJ day (that's our parents' generation) but clearly remember where we were when we heard that President Kennedy was shot. We knew the

---

[h]The song by Hank Cochran is how this book got started (it kept playing over and over in my head!), and the lines provide the chapter titles. Lyrics are on p. 127.

"Beats" before the Beatles, and longed to be "hip" before there were "hippies." So for those of you who were born before 1943 or after 1960, my apologies, but you really are a different "cat."

The Baby-boomers' values were defined by the network news, Elvis, the Beatles, Martin Luther King, and the Kennedys.[8] Then, over the next five years we watched as the political idols we'd been taught to worship were shot down, literally, one by one. Then we saw our beloved country's leaders, who we'd been taught to believe were always "the good guys," do terrible things to thousands of people in other lands – and in Washington! We began, for the first time, to see the real problems that existed in our own land – problems of poverty and hopelessness, hunger and addiction, violence and violation. And we were shocked.

Some of us literally went into shock – we withdrew from the world we saw and stayed "out of it" for years. Some of us braided flowers into our hair and went to live in communes or learn the ways of Native Americans. Some of us went into action – we became all kinds of activists, trying to undo what had been done to us, our country, and our world. Some of us went into a state of grief and mourning – an emotional state that, far too often, is diagnosed and treated as "depression."

All of us realized we had to find our way in a world that was not what we'd been taught it was, and perhaps never could be even remotely like the American Dream we'd been taught to believe in and strive for.

So we picked ourselves up, dusted off the diplomas we'd been told would be our passes into the magical kingdom of power and wealth, compromising with the system when and where we had to in order to make a life for ourselves and those we loved..

A lot of us made babies on the way, which is, at the least, a huge distraction, so we stepped off track to allow for this new experience and responsibility. Some of us figured out a way to raise

---

[8] Applying this principle to the current generation, they don't remember King or the Kennedys, but they definitely remember 9/11. So the kids born before 1997 are not the same as those born after, regardless of what the census says.

our kids and "do our work," too. Most of us gave in to the conditioning of our own childhood and bought the house with the yard and took the job to support the house and the kids for the couple of decades they needed to grow up and, hopefully, learn to function in this strange world we found ourselves living in.

Today, Baby-boomers are shocked to discover that we're not only mortgage-holding parents, but grandparents – and helping our own parents, too! Too often we find ourselves parenting our grandchildren, when their parents have collapsed into the same drugs, poverty, or depression that we were victims of. Worse, we're actually reaching an age where we may be required to retire! We're flabbergasted. This wasn't in the plan! How did this happen? Who's going to do all the work we've been doing? Carry all the burdens? And how could the world possibly be as bad off as it is, even after all these years and all this work?

We still rely on that electronic sea to tell us what's real – even more so with smart phones and internet making it a constant presence – and we still long to experience the dream of America we were taught to believe in, but now we don't have the same kind of energy and enthusiasm.

Some of us are very angry. We never did trust what we called "the establishment" and now it's clear that those people in power have betrayed us! Some of us are just plain disgusted; the American dream has become the American nightmare and we don't want any part of it. Quite a few have run off to live in other countries, finding a simpler, more harmonious life among people who still live close to the land and family.

Many of us feel (horrors!) old and tired. We just want it to be different. We want the world we've been living in to go away and we want the dream world of our childhood to become the real world for all future generations. But can it happen without a lot of pain or distress? And if so, where do we start?

Chapter 2: Get it Off
My Shoulders

The "burden of modern life"

Humanity has complained about the "burden of modern life" since the first cities were formed, over 5000 years ago. This isn't too surprising, really; human beings, however "citified," don't like to raise their families among crowds of strangers, separated from natural beauty, and governed by artificial time schedules. We have a basic need for living on our own time, feeling the warm embrace of this mothering planet's beauty, and being with the people we love. This is why people move back to the suburbs or small towns to raise their families, even if they lived the "fast life" in the city as singles and young couples. And it's why retirees are flocking by the thousands to "resort areas" where they can appreciate the beauty of the natural world while maintaining the familiar aspects of their suburban family-raising years.[9]

In the ancient cities, the visible problems were sewage and noise and the behaviors that always come when too many mammals (including people) are crowded too close together. We have commentaries ranging from Sumer to Rome filled with such complaints. And Shakespeare's *Romeo and Juliet* and Samuel Pepys'

---

[9] Oregon has long been a beautiful example of this dynamic. Portland and Eugene have, for years, had far more residents in the 20-35-year-old range than in the pre-18 and 40-60 range. Smaller towns, like Boring, Estacada, and Wilsonville, are the reverse. And in many communities on the coast and in the high desert, close to half the population is retired. Then the final decades of most Oregonians' lives are lived in the big cities again, to be close to health care and hospitals.

journals illustrate the continuation of these kinds of problems through the Renaissance era of Europe.

Throughout our "civilized" (meaning "city-based") history, anyone who could afford it has maintained a "country home" as respite from all this. Those who couldn't afford such a luxury would head to the coast or the mountains or a nearby park for a few hours of freedom every few days or a few days or weeks every year. In modern times they even buy elaborate "campers" that allow them to venture into the natural environment while carrying their civilized luxuries with them. The really poor have alsways simply numbed themselves with alcohol or drugs, sex or entertainment, and lived short, dismal lives.

A famous experiment from the 1950s illustrates the primary problem of city life. Known as "Calhoun's Rats,"[10] the experiment involved sealing off parts of a barn with lots of food and watching through viewing windows what happened as the rat population increased. At first all was well. Different families established themselves in different parts of the barn and lived a comfortable life of eating, playing, and procreating. Then, as the population increased, tensions mounted. When it got to the point where it wasn't really possible to maintain clear boundaries between one family's "territory" and another's, bands of adolescents began to rove through the barn, taking what they pleased, "raping and pillaging" in other territories, and other violent behaviors. Infanticide increased, as did spontaneous abortions, homosexuality, and various forms of stress-related illnesses. In short, the rats began to experience all the terrors of the over-crowded inner city.

Suburbs evolved in the late 1800s as a way to avoid these negative features of urban culture while still having access to the creativity of many minds working together. They offered something like the "country life" while still having access to the arts and

----

[10] This study was first described in *Scientific American*: John B. Calhoun, "Population density and social pathology" #206 (2): 139–148(1962), and later described in Edward T. Hall's *The Hidden Dimension*. (1966) New York: Anchor Books. Ch. 3.

markets and what young adults love about the city. They were initially made possible by local railroads and trolley lines. Then, with the advent of the automobile, suburbs mushroomed all around, and small towns within an hour's drive of any metropolis became "bedroom communities," where most houses were empty all day and families were only home at nights and on weekends.

This new way of living did great things for the economy as the expanding suburban population needed new houses, new appliances, new furniture, new kinds of tools and gadgets, and a regular supply of new automobiles. In the cities, the buildings these people had lived in were turned into tenements for new immigrants and those who couldn't find a way to leave, or were torn down for commercial enterprises. Lots of jobs were created, lots of money was lent, and lots of people felt very affluent.[11]

For people who lived in suburbs and bedroom communities, though, there were new kinds of problems. Surveys over the years have shown that, for suburbanites, life often feels empty and routine: the yard always seems to need mowing, the house with all its appliances always seems to need some kind of repair or upgrade, the kids are preoccupied with school, sports, and their peers, and the commute is long. Every week feels like "the same old same old." And, of course, in order to support all these benefits, the money is always tight. If there's lots of money it's because one or both of the parents are working many hours, so time for relaxing is almost unheard of. And, if one person stays home to care for the kids and the house, new problems come up: isolation, boredom, and an increasing tension around ownership and control, as is famously illustrated in the book and movie Peyton Place and the several TV series about "Desperate Housewives."

Since World War II, one constant, regardless of whether we live in cities, suburbs, or small towns, has been the electronic sea of news, music, advertising, and videos that continues to direct

---

[11] Prior to running for the presidency Donald Trump wrote a book with Robert T. Kiyosaki, author of *Rich Dad, Poor Dad,* called *Why We Want You to be Rich.* It encouraged readers to maximize their lifestyle and help the economy by maximizing their debt through investments in real estate.

our emotional and political lives. And, with the rise of the internet, the effect can be overwhelming. We hear constantly repeating reports of what the media producers decide is important news, along with selected music, in our cars, stores and offices, wherever we go, and many of us have the TV on virtually all day at home. Then, in the one room where there is no TV, we have a computer plugged into the internet telling us the current moment's news and weather, and social media informing us about what our friends and family are up to, all day every day, 24/7. We're constantly constant barraged with advertising, telling us all the things we need in order to be happy and well – now on all stations and most websites. On top of all that, most of us now have cell phones that go with us wherever we are, so we're expected to respond to whoever feels like calling us anytime and everywhere. And with "smart" phones, we're seeing those same ads and news reports, along with a constant stream of video games and other entertainment designed to help us escape the present moment.

To keep up with this constant supply, we need money. Not just the few hundred dollars a year our grandparents would raise through occasional trips to market and then use to augment what they produced at home, but thousands (and if you're a lawyer, an investment officer, or in Congress, *hundreds* of thousands) of dollars every year. Even to retire, we're told by various finance writers, people in their 30s today who want to have a retirement income equivalent to $30,000/year needs to have saved or invested over a million dollars by the time they're 65!

Part of this equation is anticipated inflation. For example, a loaf of good bread cost a nickel around 1900, $1 in the 1970s, $2 to $3 in 2000 and $3 to $5 in 2017. This means a dollar isn't worth nearly the same amount today as it was when the Baby-boomers were starting out – and *much* less than for our grandparents. It helps if we remember that the U.S. Income Tax was ratified in 1913 based on the popular belief that only the very wealthy would ever have to pay it, because they were the only ones who received over $700/year (that's about $42,000 in today's dollars – or a little less than median income in most states, today)! Nonetheless, a fine suit of clothes cost a man an ounce of gold in ancient Rome –

and still does today, so the value has not changed, though the numbers we measure it by continue to increase.

Generating the kind of cash we've been told we need to be happy and healthy means being very innovative and working very hard for most of our adult lives – or being very fortunate in one's choice of family, friends, and livelihood. If we manage to earn a lot of money in a short time, we need to find a way to "save" or "invest" it so our dollars will not be eaten up by inflation or that Income Tax that only the very wealthy were expected to have to pay when it was created. If we take a long time to earn it, we need also to find ways to "get by" on "not much" for the years it takes to accrue. Both paths require discipline and care to build our "net worth" to a level where we can feel safe and secure when the society tells us we can no longer earn a living.

So, while most of us don't take time to analyze it, Americans (and, in fact, most people in western urban industrial culture) don't feel anything like free or equal or even capable of pursuing happiness. Too many of us are "wage slaves," like the miners in the old song "You load sixteen tons and what do you get? ...deeper in debt." None of those inalienable rights to which we were born seem attainable. We feel burdened by too much debt, too much stuff, too much information, too many demands and expectations from too many people, too few resources, and too little opportunity to even figure out what makes us happy!

En-lightening Our Lives

The term enlightenment existed long before Buddhist teachings were translated into English. It was used to describe a new understanding or discovery, an opening to new possibilities that were not seen before. It can also mean to increase the amount of light, like the light-bulb that goes on over someone's head in a cartoon, as well as to lighten one's load, to reduce one's burden. Both of which, interestingly, are in line with the Buddha's[12] teaching.

---

[12] This term, "Buddha," is not a name, not a god, but a title. It means "awakened one" and describes a person who has broken out of the cultural trance and truly realizes we are not bodies driven by limited minds.

How can we "lighten our load" and see possibilities we didn't see before?

Can you imagine a world in which you feel free, equal, and able to pursue your own happiness? A world without debts and taxes? A world without social expectations that define how you live your life? Francis Bacon did in the 1600s. Jean-Jacques Rousseau, Johann von Goethe and Imanuel Swedenborg did in the 1700s. Ralph Waldo Emerson and the Transcendentalists did in the 1800s. So did Helen and Scott Nearing in the 1930s,[13] as did the hippies of the 1960s and '70s. Joe Dominguez, Duane Elgin and Sarah ban Breathnach did in the '80s, and Dave Ramsey has in this new millennium. Alongside them the New Thought teachers, including Barbara Marx Hubbard,[14] John Randolph Price[15] and Arnold Patent,[16] have imagined such a world, as well. All of these people wrote books describing their vision.

What the Buddha and Emerson and all those others knew is that our burdens, our sufferings, can be greatly lessened when we choose not to listen to the voices of the society around us. They also knew that avoiding social pressure was a difficult, almost impossible one for people whose sense of identity and well-being is tied to the opinions and actions of others.

For Emerson, the secret was to allow oneself to observe and *feel* the way that Nature works – in the world around us and in our lives. When we do so, he said, we begin to understand that we are not the product of a whimsical being, but the culmination of a magnificent, ongoing process. He said that when we begin to really know this truth, we can become the chief director of that process, but that we need to no longer let the voices of those around us drive our lives and let the Voice within us do so. That Voice, he said, has been called God, and is the Spirit and Soul of everything, including all of humanity. Once we begin to rely on

---

[13] See *The Good Life* and *Living the Good Life* by Helen and Scott Nearing.
[14] See Hubbard's *Conscious Evolution, Revelation,* and other works
[15] See Price's *Spiritual Philosophy for a New World* and other works.
[16] See Patent's books, *You Can Have It All* and *Death, Taxes, and Other Illusions*, published by Beyond Words.

that higher Self, he said, we will find that all of Nature works to ensure our fulfillment.[17]

For Helen and Scott Nearing, the answer was to leave the city and move to a farm in Vermont (and later, Maine), spending 4 hours a day working the farm and 4 hours a day writing, teaching, and publishing, for 6 days a week, and eating their own produce and local products in simple, easy-to-prepare-from-scratch meals of whole-grain cereals, fresh salads, and soups. When people who studied with them came to visit, they were put to work, too, and wonderful transformations of the land and people were the result.

For Joe Dominguez and Dave Ramsey, it's using faith and good sense to eliminate one's debts and begin to build a life rather than constantly shoveling out the hole dug by paying off loans and credit cards.[18]

For Price and Patent and all the New Thought teachers, the answer is to spend some time every day "in the Silence" to discover what inspirations and possibilities are there and to act on those possibilities, one by one, until a new life, based on that inner guidance, is formed. In the process, they say, we discover that we are not really separated from what we love and wish for, as we've always been told. The process leads us to realize that there is no separation between us and the things and people and opportunities that can bring us fulfillment, and that we truly are born free, equal, and able to pursue our own happiness. Even more, they say, fulfilling our personal happiness can never deprive another of their own happiness, because the universe – and the quantum field that pervades it and becomes all forms – is infinite.

---

[17] Emerson's essays testify to the necessity of living that kind of life. My book, *Natural Abundance: Ralph Waldo Emerson's Guide for Prosperity*, interprets those essays for the modern reader (Beyond Words/Atria, 2011).
[18] See *Your Money or Your Life* by Joe Dominguez & Vicki Robin; see also Ramsey's *Financial Freedom* or go to his class in a local church, or just listen to his evening talk-radio show.

So, what would it look like to be free of the "burden of modern life"?

At the least, it would require understanding the nature of the "burden." Historically, we can see that it's tied to the whole idea of living in and working in cities and suburbs, simultaneously overcrowded and isolated. Personally, however, we need to understand that the sense of "burden" we feel is more accurately a sense that we're "stuck with" the consequence of choices we made when we felt we had no choice. The "burden" is all the things that tell us we aren't really "free, equal, and able to pursue our own happiness."

Looking back over our lives, we can see a number of points where we did what we "had to," instead of what we believed would make us "free, equal, and able to pursue our happiness:"

➢ We "had to" go to school and get that high school diploma (and some of us "had to" finish college, too!) because "our parents made us."

➢ We "had to" register for the draft and go into the military because "otherwise they'd put us in jail."

➢ We "had to" get married, either because "we were pregnant," or because "our parents insisted," or because "we'd been dating so long, what else could we do?"

➢ We "had to" go to work and earn some money because we "had to" pay for food, clothing, and housing.

➢ We "had to" continue to work at that job even when it was no longer satisfying and we were getting sick, because "we couldn't lose the benefits."

➢ We "had to" buy the car, the house, the washing machine, the large-screen TVs, the computer, because "we need it to keep the family happy" and/or "to get our work done."

➢ We "had to" borrow money because "there wasn't any other way to get those things."

Ralph Waldo Emerson would heartily disagree. From his perspective, we didn't *have* to do any of those things; they were all choices that we made to avoid the social costs of not doing them. His neighbor and friend, Henry David Thoreau, who lived for a couple years in a cabin on the lake we know as *Walden Pond* at the back of Emerson's land, and later went to prison for what he described as *Civil Disobedience*, would concur. So would his friend Walt Whitman, who worked as a nurse during the U.S. Civil War so as not to have to kill anyone. Emerson himself lived on a small farm, raising his children and most of his food with the help of his wife, a gardener, and a cook – who all ate what they produced on that farm, making most all of it "from scratch." He paid his travel and publishing expenses with the proceeds from his writing and lectures – the work that he found most fulfilling – and he never went into debt.[19]

Even today, many of Emerson's modern followers would also disagree with our beliefs and notions. They would say that we never really "had to" do any of those things, and we definitely don't "have to" today.

If we didn't "have to" do any of these things, why did we do them and what do we do now, with the consequences of having done them?

Clearly, we did them because we believed we "had to" do them in order to survive and perhaps succeed in a world that threatened to overwhelm us with its soulless complexity. At least we convinced ourselves we did. We listened to the brainwashing by school, business, and government that our well-being depended on the accumulation of goods. Notice that word 'goods.' It assumes possessions are somehow ultimate values, not mere materials deemed necessary for us by our culture. For many of us, the idea of a choice did not exist at that time. Our minds had been carefully trained not to see anything but what was directly in front of us, so we didn't.

Now, though, like the apostle Paul, we are adults "and put away childish things." Many of us have seen that the assumptions we made in our youth were not always based on reality – in fact, they rarely were. Gershwin's song, "'Tain't necessarily so!" has become our new theme song – running in the background of all

---

[19] For a fun look at Emerson's daily life, see *Mr. Emerson's Cook* by Judith Schachner. Another glimpse may be had by reading Louisa May Alcott's *Little Women*, as Emerson was the model for the girls' wealthy neighbor.

those news and weather reports and much of what our friends, neighbors, co-workers, and family have to say.

Still, we feel stuck with the consequences and results of those choices, and many of us don't see any way out. Being trapped in a world we can't stand is the nightmare of the current generation.

This sense of being stuck is why so many self-help workshops, seminars, books, and modern gurus have emerged in our culture. We want to find a way out – a way, as the Buddhists put it, "off the wheel." So we ask questions and, being accustomed to paying for everything, buy products and experiences that, we hope, will provide them. And some of them do – so we buy more!

In fact, we're willing to put in a lot of time and effort for experiences that offer even the hope of way out.. We study how-to articles, cds, and books. As we discover the possibility of release through activity, we take up athletic pursuits, yoga, gardening, fishing, or the martial arts. We seek support in the *Bible*, the *Q'uran*, the *Sutras,* the *Vedas,* and poetry like that of Rumi. We spend hours in the spa, or in meditation and prayer. We visualize and affirm our good every day. We walk and eat right and work with one or more therapists. Afterward, we feel a little better, a little more centered, a little freer.

But when things get really scary or difficult, many of those products and experiences don't seem to help – and when that happens, when we feel like we've tried and not succeeded, we're not only disappointed, we get frustrated and sometimes angry.

If we don't believe we can express that anger directly, we may repress it until we start to show symptoms of the new national disease: depression. Having repressed this most powerful of emotions, we stop being able to feel any emotion at all, and begin to feel numb and tired and unwilling and unable to function. In this way, repression consistently leads to depression, which, in today's world, leads to medication.

If, on the other hand, we start to express our distress without limiting ourselves to "safe" situations for doing so, we may be told we're beginning to show signs of "mania" or "psychosis," which means other medications, or worse.

If we allow ourselves to be distracted from our "normal" activities by our hunger or desire for ways to get "unstuck," we may be diagnosed with "Attention Deficit Disorder" or "obsessive-compulsive disorder" and be given even yet another medication.

Clearly none of these diagnoses or treatments is addressing the real problem: our determination to be relieved of the consequences of our early choices and actions, and to feel free, equal, and able to pursue our own happiness. We vaguely remember having felt something like that when we were very small children and we want that back.

Equally clearly, a new way of thinking and acting is needed if we are to lighten our burdens, to truly "make the world go away" and feel good about life again.

Chapter 3: Say the Things...

"In the beginning was the Word..."[20]

The Power of Words

Remember "sticks and stones may break my bones, but names can never hurt me"? Did you ever really believe it? Probably not – because those names *did* hurt! They hurt us to the core of our being, like knives in our bellies or our hearts, and too often, in this age of social media bullying, lead to really disastrous results.

You've seen the look on a friend's face when someone called them something awful. That's pain! That's anger! That's all kinds of "molecules of emotion" spreading throughout the body, changing the chemistry of every cell, setting up potential for all kinds of dis-ease.[21]

Now, if we remember the look on somebody's face when they get a sincere, unexpected compliment, we see an equally powerful change – but this time, the chemicals flowing to all those cells are nourishing and empowering, and the person's health is likely to improve.

Words are, indeed, powerful!

If words can do all that, what else can they do?

More and more studies are demonstrating that the words we say and the thoughts we think affect our bodies profoundly—and the bodies around us, as well. Probably the best-known (and best-designed) studies in this area are being done by the Heartmath In-

---

[20] the book of John, 1:1
[21] For clear descriptions of this process, see Candace Pert's book, *Molecules of Emotion* or the film, *What the Bleep Do We Know?*

stitute and the Institute of Noetic Sciences. These groups have demonstrated conclusively that whenever one person thinks about someone who knows them well, both people experience changes in their brain activity, body chemistry, heart rhythms, and muscle tone – some of those changes occurring before the words are actually said – even if the two people are not in the same room! And the effects in both of them are either health-inducing or disease-encouraging depending on whether the thoughts are loving or angry/fearful.[22]

At the same time, studies show that people who repeat loving thoughts over and over for several minutes each day improve in every measure of body health, whether in vision, hearing, memory, or mental function. The degree of improvement varies. The sicker someone was, the more improvement such affirmations bring about. The more intensely they feel the thought as they repeat it, the more improvement occurs. And how frequently they repeat their loving thoughts makes for even more improvement. So if you're already pretty well and you're not too invested in the idea and you do it only a few minutes once a day, you'll see far less effect than if you've been really struggling, really feel it, and repeat the process every hour or two. This effect is the essence of Louise Hay's process, described in her book, *You Can Heal Your Life*.

A wonderful song, called "Unconditional Love" was written and sung by Greg Tamblyn two decades ago. In it he describes how Evy, confined to a wheelchair because of a nerve disease, chose to spend her days in front of a mirror and writing down all the negative thoughts that came to her mind until she could think a positive thought about herself. After a while, she stopped thinking the negative thoughts that had been her norm, and…

… a funny thing happened
when Evy decided to love herself
the deterioration stopped,

---

[22] Both have websites and newsletters documenting their results and have demonstrated some of their experiments in films like *What the Bleep, Further Down the Rabbit Hole* and *The Living Matrix*.

and then reversed itself…[23]

This is just one of millions of stories that have been written by former patients, family members, doctors, and others, documenting the effect that our thoughts and words have on our bodies, many of which are included in Jack Canfield's *Chicken Soup for the Soul* series or are available through the publishers Hay House and Atria.

Beyond the physical effect on our bodies and the bodies of those around us, though, our words have been shown to "set us up" for experiences in our relationships, our finances, our work, and our studies. This effect is why and how affirmations are encouraged – even though affirmations alone have limited effect.

What Works Better than Affirmations?

Remember when you did something really well and you knew ahead of time that "it was in the bag." You were certain it was going to be fine; there was no doubt in your mind and you told yourself, and maybe a few other people, that it was "a done deal."

Now remember a time when you didn't do so well, when you had doubts going in and felt unsure in the process, and you told yourself – or maybe someone else told you – that it was going to be tough, that you'd "be lucky to make it." Can you see the relationship between the message and the outcome?

Studies have shown that people who are told they're going to do well generally do, and those who're told they won't, generally don't. From schoolwork to athletics to music to sex, we believe what we've been told – and then we prove it to ourselves with the results we get. And it doesn't matter whether the voice that tells us is our own, or that of our parents, our coach, an announcer, or our next-door neighbor. This phenomenon is so consistent that one self-help teacher of the 1970s, Werner Erhart, used to say, "If you want to know what your beliefs and intentions are, look at your results."

---

[23] Greg Tamblyn cd *The Shootout at the I'm OK You're OK Corral*, Ramlin' Tamblyin recordings, 1991

It turns out that our subconscious mind, the part that runs our body systems, is constantly scoping the environment for opportunities to make our experience fit our beliefs. And, just like a computer or a robot, it only does what it's told – no more and no less. So, if the message it's getting is consistent, it will do only that, and if it's conflicting, it will try to do both.

This means that if I believe deep down and keep telling myself that I can write a book, my subconscious mind will make it easy for me to do that. But if I tell myself I can while believing I can't, my subconscious mind will generally make it hard for me to do so – by distracting me with "more interesting" or "more important" tasks, or causing silly errors or lost files, or any number of tricks (most of which I've experienced over the years!).

If I tell myself I can run a 3, 4, or even 5-minute mile without believing I can, it's almost guaranteed I won't. It doesn't matter how many times I try to, or how often I "affirm" it – unless I can distract my subconscious for a few minutes while I get on the track and run. The same applies to taking a test, receiving money, or speaking to a group. Motivational speaker Lisa Nichols tells a story of how this works. After coming in "dead last" during a whole season of competitive swimming, she proceeded to break the freestyle record for 18 year-olds when she was only 15 – not by affirming she could, but simply by focusing on, and repeating in rhythm, a whole new idea about who she was.[24]

By the same mechanism, if someone were to tell herself that she can cure cancer or heart disease or whatever and begins to truly believe she can, then she'll soon be doing something that causes those symptoms to disappear in the animals and people she treats – even if nobody else ever gets the same results! Call it the Placebo Effect, psychic healing, or hypnosis, it doesn't matter. As long as she believes it works and continues to let her patients believe it works, it works! In fact, when Norman Cousins cured himself of a rare illness by a series of actions no medical person believed could work, he was told it was "the Placebo Effect." He went on to be-

---

[24] Told in a lecture to a conference on *The Secret* in Toronto, Canada, published on a dvd called *The Teachers of the Secret*, by The Power Within co.

come a professor at UCLA Medical School and came to the conclusion that "the history of medicine is the history of the Placebo Effect." [25]

So what we say and what we think make a difference in our bodies, in our relationships, and in our lives. What we believe is what we *must* (can't not) experience. If we don't think we believe it, if it's unconscious, we'll experience it in dreams or in the lives and stories of people around us. If we know that it's true, though, we can be sure that it will be our experience, and soon!

Power through *the Words*

The words themselves, though, are only symbols: stand-ins for what they mean to us. For example, if I say the word "ice" to most people, they think of what's in the freezer or in their glass, or on the skating rink or sidewalk in winter. If I say it to a jeweler (or jewel thief!), however, they think of diamonds. If I say it to someone who's working outside the law, they may think I'm talking about hiding someone or something for a while, as in "putting them on ice." If I use it in reference to a person, most of us immediately have a sense of how that person relates to others. A few people will think of a form of sherbet or sorbet (as in "strawberry ice") or their favorite Hawaiian treat: shaved ice. And fans of animated films may think of the movie *Frozen*.

If you look over that set of examples again, you'll notice that each of them brings up an image in the mind – a person or a thing that has certain qualities – and maybe a memory of an experience that includes or is associated with the image. Nothing about the letters i-c-e suggests any of those images, nor is there anything about the sound of them put together. And if I used the same

---

[25] Cousins described his process in *Anatomy of an Illness,* New York: Norton, 1070. His survey of medical treatments that worked as long as people believed in them is described in *The Healing Heart: Antidotes to Panic and Helplessness*, New York: Norton, 1983. A more recent book, by Joe Dispenza, called *You Are the Placebo*, Hay House, 2014, explains how it all works.

three letters with the same sound and put an "n" or a "d" or an "r" in front of them, a whole new set of images would be evoked.

And, if I said the word *helado* (Spanish) or *glacé* (French), most Americans would just hear noise, but people from countries where those languages are spoken would think along the same lines as Americans do when we think of frozen water.

Well, if the meaning isn't in the word itself, where is it?

It's not the letters or the sound – not the word at all – that has the power. The letters can be strung together to form different words; they can be strung together in different ways in different languages to form the same word. No, it's the meaning and images that the sound evokes that communicate the information. And when this information changes our mind-systems, it has the power to change our experiences.

If I've learned some powerful affirmations – like "every day in every way I'm better and better;" or "I do wonderful work for wonderful pay and live a wonderful life in a wonderful way;" or "God works through me to will and do all that is my fulfillment to be and do;" or "*Om mane padme hum*;" or whatever – the words themselves have no power until I *give* them power by infusing them with images and feelings that are meaningful for me. Then, when I repeat them, I'm introducing a new experience into the system that is my mind, which begins to change the connections it makes. (And if I repeat them a lot for a month or so I'll change!)

So the specific words of the prayers or affirmations we use don't make the difference – it's the images and feelings that go with them. Whether we say "Father" or "Mother" or "God" or "Lord" or "Allah" or "Om" is not as important as the feeling and images that what we're saying evokes in us. Tradition has it that Jesus called God *Abba*, which is the equivalent of "Daddy," indicating a loving, nurturing relationship, which is what he taught his followers to experience. When people have experienced paternal abuse, however, they may have a negative association with God-as-Father. Their whole mental system may be shaped by the idea that God is a punishing parent. For them, another term would evoke the images and feelings that lead to the deep communion that prayer is, and that Jesus was encouraging.

For centuries, people of all religions in much of Southeast Asia have used the Arab word *Allah* and the English word *God* and the Hebrew work *Adonai* and the Greek/Hebrew word *Jehovah*, along with other words in their own languages, to refer to the one God they all share. For these people, all the many descriptors point the listener or speaker toward the image and feeling of the presence of the unnamable divine.[26] They realize that the language used is not important; the power is in the feeling that they evoke.

In my book *Uncommon Prayer*,[27] I talk about how, though the words of prayers and religious rituals are too often essentially meaningless in themselves, they're the *vehicle* by which the power is experienced. Instead of being some "magic formula" that must be said or performed in a certain way, they're the means by which we get to the state of being that is prayer. They're useful, but only insofar as they help us reach a state of consciousness where we can have the experience of "communion with the divine" – the peaceful flow of power, beauty, love, and truth – that is true prayer.

When we were children we were told there are certain "magic words" that, if used in the right way at the right time, would let us accomplish great things. *Abracadabra* was one of them. *Open Sesame* another. But, sadly, it didn't seem to matter how often or how intensely we said them – nothing wonderful ever happened.

What's faith got to do with it?

Faith is not simply a statement that you think there is only one God or that Jesus is Lord, or anything like that. In fact Jesus, among others, makes it quite clear: *faith is the certainty that what we intend to happen will happen when we do or say whatever we believe will make*

---

[26] Unfortunately, this is becoming an issue in some of those countries. New laws are saying that Christians don't have the right to refer to "their" God as *Allah*, even though both traditions are based on "The Book" – the Jewish *Torah*, which is also the Christian "Old Testament," and refer to the same Creator. Imagine being told you can't use one of the most powerful words you know in your prayers!

[27] WiseWoman Press, 2008.

it happen. Faith grows with use, with observation of results, and with repeated experience of the feeling of connection with something greater than us. Jesus, the Buddha, and saints in many traditions had faith that when they spoke, life and health would be visible where illness had been before.

In her fourth lesson, which is about faith,[28] Emma Curtis Hopkins (who taught Ernest Holmes, the Fillmores, and many other leaders of metaphysical schools and churches) called it the "confidence to command." She encouraged her students to take one morning a week to repeat the Lord's Prayer (either the traditional form or one of the new translations from the Aramaic) fifteen times, like the people at Lourdes do when they're preparing to take the healing waters. She said that this ritual is one way to "generate Faith" – that as we repeat words which evoke a feeling of connection with a Higher Power over and over, we begin to feel an increase in that power flowing in us and through us.

Then, in her next lesson, she tells us that our works are the result of that faith and not of our effort – that our "face and form" and our environments demonstrate what we have faith in. After a while, she and other healers say, we don't need to use words to transform ourselves, our lives, or the lives of others who seek us out; the power is freely accessible to us and flows through us to the person we're thinking of..

This faith, then – the kind that moves mountains and heals bodies and transforms lives – is available to all of us. That's true even though we rarely think so and as a result almost never use it.

If we'd never seen a light switch, the first few times we experienced having the lights come on when we moved this funny little plastic thing on the wall would be a miracle that we couldn't explain (not that we can really explain it, anyway!). It was impossible

---

[28] The twelve lessons of Emma Curtis Hopkins are available in all the books of which she's listed as author. Her *Scientific Christian Mental Practice* is her most detailed description of her teachings, and her *Judgment Series in Spiritual Science* is the easiest to read. My interpretation of her lessons, detailing her daily practices, is in *Unveiling Your Hidden Power, Emma Curtis Hopkins' metaphysics for the 21st century,* WiseWoman Press, 2005.

to run a mile in under 4 minutes until Roger Bannister did it, and then it became normal to do so – because now no one believes it to be impossible! The same holds true with all athletic records – and many scientific discoveries and medical "miracles," as well.

All of us have this kind of faith – we live our lives by it. We have faith that the water will run in the bathroom and the coffee-maker will produce coffee and the car or bus will get us where we're going and our clothes will stay on our bodies and protect us from the elements – and they all do, most of the time. We have faith that certain people will behave certain ways – and they do, too. We have faith that specific experiences or actions will have certain results, and so we either embrace them or avoid them, depending on whether we want those results. Werner Erhart wasn't the only teacher who said, "If you want to know what you believe, look at your results." So if you want to know what you have faith in, look at the elements of your life – the home, the work, the people, the finances, your appearance – they all demonstrate what you believe deeply enough that you are confident in depending on them.

How does that kind of faith work?

One of the more useful steps along my educational journey was a degree in cybernetics, which its discoverer, Norbert Wiener, officially defined as "the science of communication and control in living and mechanical systems."[29] The name comes from the Greek word *xybernetes*, which became *gubernator* in Latin, and "governor" in English. It's the basis of computer science, robotics, bio-engineering, and my chosen field: cultural cybernetics.

The cruise control in our cars and the thermostat in our houses (and cars) are examples of simple cybernetic systems, in

---

[29] Norbert Wiener wrote the books *Cybernetics* and *The Human Use of Human Beings* in the late 1940s. Cybernetics was developed further through a series of conferences in the 1950s, which involved people from a range of disciplines, including anthropologists Margaret Mead and Gregory Bateson, economist Kenneth Boulding, physicist Heinz von Foerster, neuropsychiatrist W. Ross Ashby, and dozens of others.

which information flows from the output to a regulator that uses the information to adjust the process so the output will meet a predetermined level (a given temperature or speed). It's called a "feedback loop." DNA and hormones regulating our bodies and the tax collector affecting our finances are more complex examples of the same mechanism. And the understanding and vision that we hold of ourselves and our world does the same thing for our mind and our experience.

In the 1960s a medical doctor named Maxwell Maltz wrote *Psycho-cybernetics* to explain how it is that what we think about ourselves and our world determines not only the choices we make but our health and the nature of our experiences. Many others have done both theoretical and experimental work in this area since, including Gregory Bateson in his *Steps to an Ecology of Mind* and *Mind and Nature*, Paul Watzlawick in his *How Real Is Real* and *Change,* and Ken Wilber's "Integral Systems," which is most succinctly described in *A Brief History of Everything.* In fact, several new fields of study, called "Constructivist Psychology," "Family Systems Therapy," "Integral Studies," "Neurolinguistic Programming," and "Phenomenological research" have emerged around these ideas.

All this work has established that our past experience strongly affects the way we perceive what's in front of us today. As Ralph Waldo Emerson put it, over a hundred years ago,

> *No man can learn what he has not preparation for learning, however near to his eyes is the object. A chemist may tell his most precious secrets to a carpenter, and [the carpenter] shall be never the wiser – secrets he would not utter to a chemist for an estate.*[30]

Emerson understood that we see and hear only what we are intellectually and emotionally prepared to see and hear.

A common theme in movies and stories is someone entering a situation so ready to experience one thing that, for a moment at

---

[30] From his essay "Spiritual Laws" found in any Emerson collection, online, or in my "translation" of some of his essays, *Natural Abundance: Ralph Waldo Emerson's Guide to Prosperity*, (Beyond Words/Atria, 2011).

least, they interpret something that's really very different – sometimes the exact opposite – as what they're expecting to see or hear. The person hears "I love you" as "I hate you," or sees a set of furniture as a wild animal or monster, or panics when some clothing falls on them because they're emotionally prepared to meet a ghost.

This re-shaping of perception works over the long term, too. If I'm mentally and emotionally prepared to experience an environment in a certain way, or to receive one kind of response from certain people, I will experience that, over and over again, even if the actuality is radically different.

An example: in one of the ministry positions I've held, a man joined the church and began offering to help on various projects. As all-too-often happens in churches, volunteers were scarce, so any offer was always appreciated and the man was included in several activities – until it became clear that, if he wasn't in charge of the activity, doing pretty much all of it his own way, and being acknowledged every moment for doing a great job, he was angry. It didn't matter how often he was thanked or how many other people were already involved or what traditions or policies were already in place. In time the staff realized that this man believed he was never respected nor really appreciated and it didn't matter how much public and private acknowledgement he received for his ideas and efforts, he would never feel adequately appreciated and would continue to resent the church staff for not "doing their job" as he saw it. The staff began to ease off on accepting his offers of help, while continuing to acknowledge and appreciate whatever he had done both privately and publicly. Not too surprisingly, he left the church in a few months.

In my own life, the "critical parent" I grew up with still shows up occasionally – either as a voice in my head telling me that what I'm doing is not "good enough," or as someone in my life saying things that I *interpret as* criticism. They may be actually complementing me, but I've heard only what I expected to hear. Clearly, I could relate to what our church member in the above example was experiencing – which fact, in itself, is an example of the principle! We really do only experience what we're prepared to take in.

Therefore, if I'm quite sure that someone will always respond the same way to something I do or say, guess what? Barring a major transformation on one of both of our parts, I will experience them as consistently doing so – even though no other observer may see it that way. And since we tend to believe that all people who remind us of that person will bhave the same way, so, by and large that, too, will be our experience.

No, I'm not "making them" behave that way; my belief is simply creating an expectation in me that they will do so. I will simply perceive what's happening in alignment with my expectation. Also, my body language and tone of voice will set up a dynamic that the other person will naturally respond to.

It almost doesn't matter what words I use, the belief behind them is the power moving the action-reaction process in both of us. If, for example, I've decided that Ms. So-and-so is unable to understand me – based on my memories of her or based on her similarity to someone from my past – then, almost no matter what is said and done, I won't experience her as understanding me. And, if I believe that her understanding me is important for my wellbeing, I may build up a hefty resentment toward her for not doing so! That resentment shows up in my tone and body-language, which confuses her so much that she really can't understand!

We see this in the media a lot. It's often woven into comedy, as some character – a butler, a master teacher, a "dumb blond" or other stereotype – responds the same way to everything a main character does or says no matter how much the character changes those actions or words.

If my experience is what I have faith in, what do I do if I don't like what I'm experiencing?

The process of changing an experience of interaction among a group of people is the essence of Family Systems Therapy. It's based on the principle that our interactions with the people around us are functioning as a system consisting of:

➤ whoever's interacting,

> ➢ the beliefs and expectations of everyone in the interaction, and
> ➢ the natural tendency to simply flow with those expectations.

As with any system, when any of those elements changes, the whole system is different, and the old pattern of behavior ends. Again, it's not the specific words we use; it happens *through* the words, the feelings and images that are experienced with them.

If I want to change the system, then, I simply shift one of the elements.

Applying this approach to the problem of being misunderstood, if I make a point to document every time I am *understood*, every time I see that someone is understanding what I'm saying, I'll begin to change my expectations and behavior, simply by the process of observing them, and I'll see others' responses in a new way. Or, if I can allow myself to imagine that Ms. So-and-so – and everyone like her in my past – not only understands me but supports my well-being, and if I can interact with her while I'm feeling that possibility, then I may be very surprised at how much she really does understand!

Because I'm now operating from a different perspective, even if I do or say very much the same thing I've always done or said to her before, Ms. So-and-so will respond to the power of my new belief, with its associated tone and body-language, very differently. She'll either respond with much more understanding, or I'll see that she's always understood but I didn't see it before. Or, if we truly can't see eye to eye, she'll simply stop showing up; she won't be in my world at all – and someone else, who can easily understand me, will show up in her place.

The effect of this kind of systemic change will last as long as I operate from the new belief. If, for some reason, I revert to the old beliefs and behaviors, I can count on the world around me to respond in the same old way.

You've probably had this experience already – or seen it in a movie or TV show. It's a common theme in "coming of age" stories like *Beauty and the Beast, Secondhand Lions,* or *The Man with No Face* or TV series like *Touched by an Angel.* Someone in your life was really uncomfortable to be around; you and others may even have been a little afraid of them. Then you learn something about their history; something about why they behave that way, and your thinking about them shifts from "they're awful" to compassion for their situation. Then, all of a sudden, this terrifying or belligerent person becomes someone with gifts to offer. Lots of love stories start with people hating each other based on some misunderstanding, then each discovering who the other person really is and so transforming their belief system – and the relationship.

This is how the old world is ending! Hooray!

Chapter 4: I'm Sorry...

When we were growing up, our parents and other adults would require us to say "I'm sorry" whenever we did something they didn't like or didn't think was "nice." They thought they were teaching us how to behave in polite society and how not to act in hurtful ways.

We also were taught to use those words as sympathy. "I'm sorry you had that happen to you..." or "I'm sorry to hear that," was what we heard adults say and learned to say, ourselves.

That teaching, however, had two unfortunate side effects. First, we began to believe that we were, indeed "sorry." Part of us began to think that we were not good enough, not smart enough, not strong enough to prevent the problem. Then, when we heard or read about someone being a "sorry little thing" or some such character, we took it on. So, deep inside most adults is a very sorry child, sad and worn and just not good enough, which is not the healthiest or most compassionate way to view ourselves.

Second, the words "I'm sorry" became virtually meaningless to us. We used them too often for what seemed to us to be relatively meaningless actions, so when big things came along, neither we nor the person we hurt were satisfied with a simple "I'm sorry," much less "my bad." It just wasn't good enough, not "big" enough, to undo the hurt. There was no power left in the words. They changed nothing.

Forgiveness as Giving-for-ness

The same thing happened with "I forgive you." Or "you're forgiven." How do words that applied to accidentally bumping into someone, or not being somewhere on time, or not sharing what we have in an appropriate way, also apply to broken hearts or

41

bones – or homes? Worse, how could words that imply that we, or someone else, did something wrong undo the wrong?

Again, the words themselves are not important. Neither the sounds nor the letters that make them up have the power to do – or undo – anything. As we discovered with the word "ice" in the previous chapter, every language has their own version and, if we don't know the language, the words are empty sounds.

However, whether we know their language or not, someone who is truly giving or seeking forgiveness can get their *meaning* across to us, and that's what we're all looking for. It is, in fact, a powerful experience, one that can transform our lives.

I came to understand this when reading *Something More* by Catherine Marshall. In the 1940s, she was sent to bed with severe symptoms of TB, which dragged on for years. The wife of a minister she used spiritual as well as medical resources to help her heal, but recovered only when she looked back over her life and wrote letters of forgiveness to each and every person she held anything against – and also letters asking forgiveness. Some of those letters could not be mailed, since the people were no longer living in their bodies, so she burned them as a way to send her message to their souls. Her recovery was prompt and complete. She was given health and vitality in return for her anger and distress.[31]

Emma Curtis Hopkins tells us in her third lesson teaching people to become healers,[32] that the idea of "forgiveness" is actually a "giving-for-ness." We're letting go of something and being given something for it. She says that if we've felt hurt about something someone has done or said, we can hang on to it and continue to experience the pain of it, or we can release it, empty ourselves of the feelings, and open ourselves to more love and life

---

[31] This process is portrayed in the film *A Man Called Peter,* with Richard Todd and Jean Peters, 1955.

[32] The 12 lessons of Emma Curtis Hopkins are in all her books. Her *Scientific Christian Mental Practice* is her most detailed description of her teachings, and her *Judgment Series in Spiritual Science* is the easiest to read. My "translation" of her lessons, with her daily practices, is *Unveiling Your Hidden Power, Emma Curtis Hopkins' metaphysics for the 21st century,* WiseWoman Press.

and potential – which is given to us for what we've released. For her, it's not about what we say to someone else, at all!

In *A Course in Miracles*,[33] we're taught that forgiveness is essential to our well-being and the well-being of others, and that true forgiveness is what makes miracles happen. According to the *Course*, "there is no order of difficulty in miracles," which is to say, miracles that affect a whole community or planet are no more difficult than ones that bring us a parking place or heal a relationship. So, when we think of or are reminded of someone and *all we can remember is the love between us*, then forgiveness has happened and not only are both of us free, but the entire world is closer to being restored to wholeness. Now that's power!

How can I find a way to forgive like that?

The key to forgiveness is to realize that the past is not real now but is only a memory, and the future does not yet exist– it's only a fantasy.[34] Now, right this moment, as I sit here or stand here or take the next step in front of me right now, I am alive and well and have enough of all that I could need for this moment.

When I know these things, I can release the past, letting it go because I realize it doesn't really affect me now, in this moment, ever. Then I can embrace all the beauty, joy, and possibility of this present moment without dragging the past into it. I've been given the joy of this moment in return for releasing the pain of the past. And, when I think of someone without bringing up that old stuff, all I remember is the love between us.

All the parables in the *New Testament* along with all the exercises that Hindu and Buddhist teachers offer or are in Emma

---

[33] *A Course in Miracles* was the inspired writing of two atheistic Jewish psychiatrists in the 1960s, who'd been seeking solutions to the difficulties they were having at work. Over several years, one of them would wake up each day and "hear" words to be written down. She'd bring them to work and the other would type them up and edit them. They ended up with over 800 pages of manuscript with daily lessons and explanatory texts, which were later published by the Foundation for Inner Peace.
[34] This is also the message that Eckart Tolle provides in his book, *The Power of Now*.

Hopkins' work or *A Course in Miracles* are designed to help us reach that state of joy and peace.

Releasing the Past

Now when we say "let go of the past," we're not saying "pretend it didn't happen." No, that way brings all kinds of problems. What we're really saying is to find a way to no longer attach any meaning, or feel any energy, or have any emotional response to the memory. Remember, *it's the meaning and images* evoked by the word (or memory) that change our experiences.

Memory is a fascinating process. The mind works by association, so if we smell a turkey roasting we remember past Thanksgivings, or a certain perfume recalls a certain person, or the smell of medicinal alcohol puts us back in a doctor's office or hospital, or the smell of liquor on someone's breath may put us back into a painful childhood situation. If we see certain colors, patterns, or profiles, we have the same kind of experience.

If we hear songs or sirens or brakes screeching or children laughing, our memories bring the past into the present and we relive moments that have nothing to do with what's going on here and now as if they were actually happening here and now. It's the mechanism of Post-Traumatic Stress Disorder (PTSD), when someone who has been through a major trauma finds themselves reliving that trauma and bringing all the emotions, energy, and fear associated with it to whatever is happening, now.[35]

A similar pattern occurs if someone has been sexually abused. It will affect all their relationships, thereafter. Each subsequent experience of physical intimacy sends the abused one back to the original experience. If, however, those who have been abused can release the emotional response felt when remembering the event or the person, they can be more present to the current situation. If they can "release the past" they can have the joy of the present instead of constantly reliving the painful past.

---

[35] The PTSD phenomenon, and an effective response, is beautifully illustrated in an episode of the tekevision series *The West Wing*, called "Noel"

How can anyone "release" a past event, especially one that really hurt us?

Such a shift is what all the exercises in Emma Hopkins' works, the 12-step programs, *A Course in Miracles,* and many therapies are designed to do. During my own healing process I put to-together a synthesis of all these methods that's worked for me and dozens of students and clients. It's written up in detail in a book I co-authored a few years back, called *Calm Healing,*[36] but here's the summary version.

➢ Awareness – seeing that something (an idea, belief, situation, story, person, behavior) in our experience doesn't fit with what we know or intend our lives to be – it doesn't feel good.

➢ Acceptance that this something-that-doesn't-fit is, in fact, part of our experience and past sense of self (rather than pretending it's not).

➢ Acknowledging that, while it doesn't feel good, it has served a purpose in our lives, if only to bring us to this state of being in this moment.

➢ Expressing the full range of feelings that come up when we look at the something-that-doesn't-fit – literally "pressing out of, or pushing from" our being, our bodies, our emotional center, our intellect, all the feelings, words, images, thoughts, songs, movements, that are associated with this experience, through writing, speaking, dancing or other movement, music, pounding on pillows, and other safe modes of expression – alone, where others will not be affected.

➢ Releasing all of that – burning papers we've written on, filling a virtual "garbage bag" and tossing it, showering it down the drain, imagining someone carrying it away, or whatever works – to let the psyche know that this is no

---

[36] "Twelve Steps to Freedom," in *Calm Healing, methods for a new era in medicine*, by Robert Bruce Newman and Ruth L. Miller, published by North Atlantic Books, 2006.

longer a part of our self-image. (I like stuffing it all into an imaginary rocket ship and sending it into the sun to be transformed into healing light; one person put it in a hot-air balloon and watched it drift away; others ask angels, *devas*, or Christ to take it away; one man's "self-consuming" garbage bag is a delight!)

➢ For-giving – following the release process, getting to an internal space where we can tell all the people involved that we've let go of this and no longer hold them responsible for their part in it; as we imagine them in front of us we then ask them to release/forgive us for holding/blaming them for our experience; and in that space of shared release, we can then accept that there is no blame/judgment from "on high" and step into a delightful state of grace in which all that exists is the love and light between us.

➢ Claiming/Declaring – in that state of grace is power, and we focus it by claiming/accepting a truer idea of our being/experience/relationship.

➢ Affirming – writing and speaking this new idea frequently, practicing it, and, when any old habits of thought/action are triggered, canceling them and replacing them with this new one.

That's it! It can take seconds, hours, or weeks, depending on our willingness, attachment, and focus. It's demonstrated its effectiveness hundreds of times over the 20+ years I've been using and teaching it – typically removing about 80% of whatever emotional "charge" is attached to the "something" each time it's done.

Then, some time – weeks, months, or even years – later, when we start having emotional reactions to similar events, we do it again – removing another 80% (for math-lovers, we now have 4%) of the duration and intensity of the emotional reaction, and freeing us from the experience's effects for another extended period of time. If it comes up again, we may feel like we've gotten nowhere, but we do the process again. It takes much less time and effort and we remove another 80%. At this point we're down to .32% of the original event's duration and intensity and, if we experience the trigger event again, we hardly notice it.

How often do we need to do a process like this?

When his student, Peter, asked that question, Jesus said "seventy times seven" which is an idiom meaning, "as often as it takes." Usually, it takes just a couple more times through the experience and process to be fully free of any emotional effects of the original event.

We know we're free when three things are different:

1. we're no longer attracting more of the same experience – we go for months, even years, without ever seeing someone or something that reminds us of it;
2. we're no longer upset or reacting in the way we used to when we do have a similar experience;
3. we no longer feel anything other than loving appreciation for the people involved – we see how they helped us learn something or get through or beyond something or were simply trying to love us in the only way they knew how.

From Atonement to At-one-ment

When we do this process (or anything like it) there's a point where we no longer feel anger, upset, or hatred toward the people who "hurt" us – we're no longer upset at the people who were involved in the event or who reinforced the false teaching or who prevented us from being our own selves. All those emotions have been drained from our being, and we feel nothing toward them or anyone else.

At this moment the atonement is really possible. In this moment we can imagine them in front of us as faces from the past without feeling any particular emotions toward them. Now, we can tell them we no longer hold anything against them and ask them to do the same for us – and, because we no longer hold anything against them, we can finally feel the love they've been trying to express toward us all along.

This is what atonement is all about: being able to be together without the past getting in the way. It's brothers and sisters making up and forgetting they ever had a fight, or lovers falling in love all over again. It's mothers and daughters delighting in what they have in common; fathers and sons sharing a new level of comfort with each other. It's determined enemies becoming best friends, at-one with each other in love. It's one world ending so another can begin.

What's happening when we do this?

In that moment all those habitual thoughts and stored up emotions are gone; they're meaningless, part of an empty past. Some people never can remember them again, except perhaps under hypnosis.

In that moment, even if we never actually are in the physical presence of the other person, we know we're both changed. The system that is our relationship has been transformed.

In that moment, once we get over the surprise, we open up a totally different kind of relationship between us and them, and between us and the rest of the universe (or God or Higher Power or Christ or Goddess or *Brahman*). As we release and allow releasing – forgive and allow forgiving – we shift into a new level of being in which the conscious energy that is the universe flows into, around, and between all of those involved.

I experience it as a "cone of light" that surrounds and enfolds both of us in that imaginary space where release is complete. And, in that "cone of light" there's a new kind of power. *A Course in Miracles* calls it "the state of grace." It's a wonderful state to be in, calm and energizing at the same time. (In fact, I've been working through this process as I write, and I've been enjoying that state for several minutes, now! It's marvelous!)

In that state, inspirations are possible that could not get through our emotional barriers before. In that state, we realize the loving guidance that's been working in our lives all the time – and the power that's available to us, always.

In that state, we *feel* the freedom that is our birthright. The people and experiences we were releasing begin to fade from our awareness and we simply enjoy the light, love, and freedom we're experiencing.

Then, at some point, we know. We know what belief and understanding we're ready to live from, now. Some words and phrases, but most importantly, some *feeling* associated with those words, comes into our awareness. (For me, right now, it's a line from *A Course in Miracles*, "all that exists is the love between us!") And that feeling, cued by those words, becomes our claim for our lives, our *mantra*, our constant affirmation.

What has happened in that state is a momentary glimpse of what Hindus and Buddhists call *Samadhi*, and Jesus called "the Kingdom." It's the state of being in which there is no separation between us and the "love-bliss-consciousness" (*satchitananda*, Christ-Consciousness, "the Beloved," God) that is woven into and through and expressing/manifesting as the universe we experience. That moment is our own personal establishment of Heaven on Earth – the world we've known is starting to go away, to be replaced by something more like Heaven on Earth.

In that state there's no more thought that God is "out there" and we are "separate from That." We experience the Truth of 'I AM That'! Any idea of separation is wiped away The act of "atonement" that made it possible for us to release part of our past becomes an experience of "at-one-ment" with the Source and Power and Presence of All That Is.

In that moment, the world we were living in, with all the distress associated with those memories, has ended and a new one is beginning. And we're so glad!

And so it is, always.

Chapter 5: If I Hurt You

The Experience of Pain

Most of us were taught that feeling pain and being hurt were part of being human. Some of us were told that we have to feel pain in order to experience joy. Now isn't that a wonderful justification for misery! Some of us were even told that we would learn better if we felt a little pain – another remarkable justification that has no basis in reality!

In fact, the belief that "if you spare the rod, you will spoil the child", though reinforced for centuries, is based on the false notion of fear as a primary motivation. Consistent proof that rewards work much more effectively than punishment was perhaps the greatest gift of behavioral psychology, a field of research developed in the 1950s. And since then, the field of neuropsychology has shown that the learning process is, in itself, rewarding to the body-mind. So there's another belief we can release!

Like most Baby-boomers, I've been fascinated with how the mind works since I can remember, I took a bunch of psychology courses as an undergraduate, and more in graduate school. I read everything I could get my hands on, and, though lack of finances kept me from becoming as "seminar junkie" I learned as much as I could about popular methods of mind development.

So it was that in the early 1970s I was first learning to shift out of my normal, verbal, thinking awareness into a state of consciousness that was primarily visual. I discovered that many of my "normal" aches and pains went away when I did so. My reading about consciousness and meditation showed me that many people had similar experiences. I began to practice withdrawing my awareness from various parts of my body and into a place at the center of my skull, a place of "empty fullness, "light darkness." I learned later that the practice of *kriya yoga*[37] involves a similar activity. My near-constant headaches were relieved and the "leg aches" that I associated with being overly tired didn't bother me anymore.

Then, when I was pregnant, I practiced the LaMaze techniques[38] to get through labor and delivery. The special breathing practices and a "focus of attention" that training offered, combined with my previous techniques for withdrawing awareness from the body, made labor easier, but the doctors decided a Caesarean Section was needed, so I didn't get to practice through delivery. Instead, I got to practice them through the aftermath of major abdominal surgery – to the point where one of the nurses came to me after a couple of days and apologized because she hadn't realized that I'd had a C-section. Because I was relatively comfortable she hadn't done all she would have done for a "normal" patient recovering from having her belly sliced open.

I wouldn't say I have a high tolerance for pain, because I know for a fact that this body responds instantly and with great distress to all cuts, breaks, bruises, rashes, inflammations, and needles seen or felt. What I have learned, however, is that I don't have to experience the symptoms as hurting – and in so doing, I can reduce the symptoms and their effects.

So I came to understand that feeling pain was neither necessary nor even helpful. And I learned to work *with* the body, instead of fighting it, whenever distressing symptoms or events occurred.

---

[37] The Self-Realization Fellowship, an outgrowth of the work of Paramahansa Yogananda, teaches the Kriya Yoga method, which is introduced in Yogananda's *Autobiography of a Yogi*.

[38] Fernando Lamaze was an obstetrician in France in the 1940s when he saw that midwives were able to assist women through labor with less pain than the then-prevalent medical model. He introduced breathing and focusing techniques, as well as exercises, that reduced the length and intensity of the labor experience. Marjorie Karmel experienced his methods while in France and described them in her 1959 book, *Thank you Dr. Lamaze!* which has recently been reprinted.

How's tolerating pain different from not experiencing it as painful?

In the opening scenes of the classic movie, *Roadhouse*, Patrick Swayze's character, a bouncer, gets into a knife fight. When it's all over, he picks up his "kit," goes into the washroom and stitches up the cut (even to write that gives my body a nervous reaction!). A few days later, a doctor observes the "good job" and asks who did it. Understandably, she's surprised when he says he did, and she says that it must have hurt. In response, he says "Pain don't hurt."

"Pain don't hurt." What a concept! Athletes and dancers train themselves to keep on going *through* the pain, focusing on the goal at hand.[39] Then they get treated, after the event is over. Soldiers have gone through a whole military operation, focusing on the task at hand, only to discover later that they were wounded.

How can we reduce the hurt?

One of the first lessons taught in LaMaze childbirth classes is to relax all the muscles in the body and then let one muscle be tense. The woman makes a fist while keeping everything else relaxed or lifts one leg while the rest of the body is relaxed. Long, slow, deep breaths help keep the muscles relaxed, and focused intention lets the one part be tense. The aim of the training is to allow the uterus to contract without tensing the whole body, which is our normal reaction but can be so tiring that the whole process becomes more painful.

Besides breathing and relaxing, LaMaze encourages us to focus on something outside of our body so we're not putting our attention on the muscles that are contracting. This idea is similar to the "self-hypnosis" approaches to pain control—where people who are going to the dentist (or whatever) are encouraged to let their minds "travel" somewhere else while they're in the chair, so

---

[39] There's a story that, in the scene at the end of the movie *Dirty Dancing*, Patrick Swayze jumped off the stage – and broke his ankle! But kept on dancing with a smile on his face... I guess he really understood that "pain don't hurt!"

their attention is not on the experience their body is going through.

So, my first response, when something physical or emotional calls for my attention, is to breathe—long and slow, deep and re-laxed. I consciously relax every part of my body while whatever is happening happens. This means that, when the dentist hands me a ball to hold on to, or I'm encouraged to grip the arms of the chair, I refuse, and hold my hands open on my lap: a signal to my body to relax.

The second response is to focus on something else: some-thing pleasurable or, at the least, elsewhere. This is common advice for dental patients or anyone seeking to avoid an uncom-fortable situation. I usually pick a favorite vacation spot and imagine I'm there: feeling the air, seeing the colors, hearing the sound, smelling the smells.

My third process comes from a variety of places, but mostly from training as a *Reiki* practitioner in the 1980s. *Reiki* is a method for allowing "universal life energy" (which is what *reiiki* means) to flow through us and into the bodies of others, as they request it. It was developed in Japan by a Dr. Usui, who was blending Buddhist and Christian ideas as a way to bring health to the poorest of the poor after World War II. Most of the method is simply to become quiet and allow the energy that supports our own aliveness (known in China as *chi* and in Japan as *ki,* in India as *prana*, and among Christians as the *Holy Spirit*) to flow into us and through our hands into the body of someone in front of us.

One of the methods I was taught involves "seeing" light flow through another person's body to help find blocks to be undone. This process begins with imagining that it might be possible to see the *chi* or *Reiki* energy as a form of light. Then we overlay that im-agining on the body of the person in front of us, letting it take on a life of its own. If they don't censor themselves; it's remarkable how accurately most people are in observing (intuiting?) the places where the person they're focusing on has been having difficulty.

Part of every *Reiki* practitioner's training is to direct the ener-gy to various parts of our own body. It's been years since I've given my body a *Reiki* treatment, but I do periodically visualize a shower of the energy of life flowing through all the cells of this body – especially if any of them are complaining or aren't functioning harmoniously with the others.

As a result of using these techniques, I've not felt the need for (or used) pain-killers or anti-inflammatories (prescription or over-the-counter) for over 20 years, even after significant surgeries or injuries. I'm guessing that Patrick Swayze's character ('the name is Dalton") in *Roadhouse* did something similar.

But what about emotional pain? What about that deep hurt that no painkillers can touch?

After I typed these words I took a short break and walked past my family's rather extensive video collection, where *Good Will Hunting* called my attention. Talk about deep hurt! Nothing that boy did could ease his suffering. Not drinking, fighting, or working himself into oblivion, not absorbing every book in the Boston Public Library and talking down grad students and professors. Even being with the woman he loved only seemed to calm it for a little while.

It wasn't until someone who suffered from an equally deep pain made him face it, feel it, and own it – and then absolve his guilt – that he was freed. (The role of the therapist who saw that and helped him through it was probably Robin Williams' best performance ever!)

It's always fascinated me how two people can grow up in the same family and have totally different memories, or totally different emotional responses to their childhood. How is it that one kid grows up as a semi-outcast in the inner city, with no father, no real support at school, not nearly enough food, clothing, or adequate shelter, and becomes a lawyer, minister, doctor,[40] or motivational

---

[40] An example that leaps to mind is Dr. Ben Carson, son of an illiterate single mom who grew up in the inner city and went on to become a leading pediatric neurosurgeon, wrote a couple of books, had a movie made about his life (*Gifted Hands*), and ran for U. S. president – then was appointed the U.S. Secretary of Housing and Urban Development.

speaker, while a dozen others end up in jail or dead! Sometimes they're from the same household! How can this be?

Many people say that it's a function of "temperament," that some of us are born with a tendency to be strong and optimistic and others are born to "follow the crowd" or see the "glass half empty." (In my experience authorities in type-defining fields like astrology, Enneagram, or genetics are most likely to say so.) And yet, some of these kids seem to follow one path for a while and then turn around and live a very different kind of life. Malcolm X may be the prime example of that process, but there are thousands of others, including many Christian and Hindu saints.

There are people who say our behaviors and emotional responses are a function of birth order or what the family system was as they were growing up. Yet some of the most successful people were first, some middle, and some the last to be born, and, with single, working, uneducated moms and absent dads, most of their family systems weren't likely very different.

Of course, individual experiences along the way can make a difference. One child may have had a supportive teacher for a term – but then so did all the other kids in that class. One child may have had a supportive grandparent, aunt, or uncle – but then so did all the others in that family.

No, I've come to understand that the kids who break out of the trap of poverty and pain are the ones who, like Will Hunting, look at their pain, own it, feel it, and find a way to be absolved from it. They may do it in jail, in a foster home, in reading a book or seeing a movie, in a job, in a physical or emotional trauma, in a church, in their love for another person, or (as for Will Hunting) in someone else's loving commitment to their well-being. For one powerful moment they realize that the life they've been living, with all its pain, is not the life they were born to live. They get that they have the option to choose another way of being – and they take it.

The same applies to those middle-class kids who experienced the abuse, neglect, and abandonment that often comes with suburban life. Or the wealthy kids who experienced the same, plus the added pain of being treated as an object – or as someone who can be "bought off" rather than loved.

For me, the pain of the past began to loosen its hold when I began to use the process outlined in Chapter 4, above.

The Source of the Experience

Feeling pain, being hurt, is something we're trained to experience. Some of us "unlearn" it and become athletes and dancers. Some of us find ways through it to live more comfortable lives. Some of us make a career of it. And why not? In our culture, one can!

Have you ever watched a baby learn to walk? It's fascinating. They toddle along, intent on the process or whatever they're headed toward, and then suddenly, they're down! If they're still intent on their object, they just get up and keep going. If, however, someone has recently swept in and picked them up and cuddled them after such a fall, you can see them take a look around and decide whether it's time to cry for attention or not. If it appears no one's looking, they'll usually get up and keep moving. But if they think someone's watching, they'll screw up their face and get ready to yell – until and unless something more interesting catches their attention.

By and large, babies who are allowed to have their own experiences in a safe space are much more independent and much less inclined to scream for help when things don't go as they anticipated – all the way through to adulthood.

By the same token, babies who are reinforced for being upset or hurt whenever they fall or don't get what they want are far more insecure and far more likely to scream for help in a wider range of situations. And, as they grow up, their distresses are more and more reinforced: they get sick and get special attention; they fail at school or sports and get special attention; they're misunderstood by people around them and get special attention; they break the rules or laws and they *still get special attention*. All this, even though behavioral psychologists proved in the 1950s that you can't stop someone else's behavior by paying attention to it – you have to withdraw attention from the undesirable behavior and focus attention on every event of the desired behavior!

The farming families of previous generations (and even today, in other countries) understood this principle and pretty much let their children have their own experiences in relatively safe spaces. But too often parents living in urban and suburban areas that they don't consider to be safe haven't figured that out – or how to implement it – and schools and daycare centers are too concerned about lawsuits to follow it. As a result, urban- and suburban-raised children have generally been raised by the "attention-to-hurts" approach. Once, only a few well-to-do children (as in the book and films, *The Secret Garden)* or over-protected urban children had this experience. The Baby-boomers were the first generation of our culture to experience such practices as the norm, regardless of income, and since then, we've had several generations of babies who were trained to get loving attention by hurting.

On top of that, there's the ongoing "electronic sea" drowning us in story-lines and song-lyrics about being hurt and being loved to remove the hurt. These songs and stories have saturated our memories and permeated our cells with the idea that we will be, are being, and have been hurt, and only someone else's love can make us feel better.

We've been taught, therefore, to expect to be hurt and to expect to experience love as a result. So, effectively, we go around wearing signs that say "I hurt; please love me!" or "Hurt me so I'll feel loved." And, if someone shows up without such a sign, we think they're showing off – trying to make us feel bad – or there's something wrong with them: surely they must hurt; they just don't know it!

So, sadly, many people think that talking about what's hurting, or will hurt, or used to hurt, is appropriate social "small talk." They play a game that Eric Berne called "Ain't it Awful?" in his book *Games People Play*, back in the 1970s. The object of the game is to be the one with the biggest problem. The sad result of playing it is that the things we don't like about our lives become the focus of our conversations – which, through the power of the spoken word, encourages our mind-body system to make more of those things happen in our lives.

Too many of us have become the victims of the meaning and images we've portrayed in our "small talk." Whenever we have joked about pain or about a possibly distressing future, we've been reinforcing beliefs about who we are and how the world works. These, in turn, have then been reinforced by new experiences that we have unknowingly created or attracted to ourselves by the very words we have spoken and images we've held in mind.

How can it be our fault when someone does something hurtful?

There's really no blame or fault here. However, as we saw in Chapter 3, above, if we expect people to behave a particular way toward us, even if we're not aware that we're expecting it, they will tend to do so. They'll behave that way for two reasons:

1. we've actually encouraged them into our experience by our belief that people could behave that way toward us; and
2. our thoughts, words, and behavior encourage it, even if we think we don't want it.

And this most definitely applies to the experience we call "being hurt."

This truth is why most spiritual teachers, including Jesus, tell us we can't really be victims. We are a participant in the process in which we were hurt – and then we've blamed the other for hurting us. The power (as always!) is in our belief, which comes *through* our words and actions.

Is Relief Possible?

When we've spent our lives living according to one pattern of beliefs and experiences, it usually seems almost impossible to shift out of them. But, as we saw earlier, *we can change our feelings* about the past, which then offers us a different kind of experience in the present – and the future.

How can we start the shift?

For most of us, it takes a major trauma – sometimes in the form of a diagnosis that terrifies us – to serve as our "wake up call" and motivate us to do what's necessary for relief from our past patterns.

The process outlined in Chapter 4, above, was developed in the late 1980s in response to my own need to end the physical and emotional consequences of living from the pain and "programming" of years past. I was going through a several-month period of intense physical pain and increasingly damaging physical symptoms, which, at that time, didn't fit any diagnostic model and so, I was told, were "untreatable" and probably terminal. I had just completed the Ph.D. and was the mother of pre-adolescent girls; I was not ready to leave this life.

Once I accepted those two possibilities: that my body symptoms were untreatable by normal methods and I wasn't ready to leave the planet, I was in a position to do something.

I had studied psychology and worked with therapists; I had studied religion and worked with spiritual counselors; I had studied meditation and worked with "self-help" gurus; I had studied shamanism and done experiments in consciousness. Through the help of friends, I learned to provide *Reiki* for myself and others. And nothing I found fixed the problem – though all of it was useful.

When no one outside of me seemed to have a solution, I went inside. After being alone for several days (for the first time in over a decade), I began to be guided by a loving inner Voice, to do only what I felt guided to do from the inside. I reviewed all the healing models I had studied. Then, with the help of a new kind of therapist who understood that physical ailments were closely related to emotional experiences, I began to undo the ties to the past that were killing me in the present.[41]

I knew that "I'm sorry" and "I forgive you" were now empty words for me, but it was clear that, somehow, what they stood for

---

[41] A description of that experience may be found in my book *Finding the Path,* published by WiseWoman Press.

had to happen. I saw that "atoning" or "making amends" was important, but that going through the motions wasn't good enough, and that often the people I needed to do the work with were no longer available to do it. I saw that expressing my upset at someone else was useless, even potentially harmful, and expressing it in an empty room simply left an emptiness inside me—and that, usually, all that I'd just expressed would simply tumble right back into that emptiness. I saw that affirmations were an important way to keep my attention focused on where I wanted to go, but that simply "affirming" my desires without clearing out the blocks to their fulfillment could not work.

What's the first step?

When I was realizing that healing the body required a radical change in my thinking, it was clear that there was value in all of the processes I had studied and that there must be a way they could be used together to make a difference. The "12 steps" framework seemed most consistently effective in transforming lives, so I started with that first step: #1 Accept that there's a problem…Then, as I moved through the steps I added various tools that I knew to be effective, and so developed the process described in Chapter 4.

As I worked through that process the first time, I thought it was going to kill me. I had never allowed myself to feel all the anger and resentment and hurt that I'd been storing in my body and memory all those years. And when I was done, I didn't think I'd ever move again; I was so drained!

Then I found myself saying things like "and I know you thought you were doing the best… I know you were trying to love me… I wish it could have been different…" At that point, all I could do was release the whole thing. I let out a big breath and relaxed, remembering words like "Let go and let God;" "Turn it over to the Spirit;" "Release it to the elements." I was done in.

As I did so, though, I began to feel a new energy. I lifted myself off the floor and began to tear up all the papers I'd written on, and then was energized enough to set up a way to burn them. I looked around the room and "saw" a mist over everything, realized it was all the emotional energy I'd filled it with, so, amazed that I could, I got up and "scooped it all up" into a virtual "paper bag" and used the transforming flames of the fire to disperse it as love and light. I watched the flames and let myself feel the light inside me, as well. I watched the smoke and felt my spent emotions transformed and dispersed with it.

Then I could use the word "forgive." Then I knew I was done with all that I had held on to – even though I hadn't realized I was holding on to it! I imagined each person and said the words: "I forgive you; I release the block between us; it's done; we're both free." Then, for the first time in months, maybe years, I no longer felt the pain—either emotional or physical.

Relief was possible. I had proved it. And it has proved itself over and over again, for me and for many others, over the years.

Pain-Free? Really?

How wonderful to be able to live without pain! How beautiful the world is when we can open our eyes and hearts to it! …How frustrating to feel it all dissolve again into the old pattern of pain and distress!

Yet, for most of us, that's what happens. We do the work, we release the past, we allow ourselves to really experience the wonders of the present, we start doing new and interesting things… then someone or something shows up and we feel ourselves being sucked back into that old morass again.

Fortunately, we have tools. We know the process; we can do it again. And again. And each time we do, the pain is less intense and lasts a shorter time. Finally, we have the delightful experience of observing the person or the activity or the event that used to send us into distress going right on by with no effect at all. Hooray! It's done!

For most of us, most of the time, this is all it takes. Over a period of weeks or months (and occasionally years, with long intervals of freedom in between) we work through the cycles until the pattern no longer affects us. We've removed the energy from the experiences that led to the pattern so we no longer repeat the pattern. We're done.

Sometimes, though, we need to go deeper. Sometimes what we're working with is not just a set of experiences or memories that led to beliefs or decisions we made about how the world works. Sometimes it's an event or series of events in our own lives – or in the lives of the people we care about – that's almost in our genes; it needs to be addressed in a different way.

Can anyone really "un-do" the past? How can we change reality?

Recently, a new form of therapy, called "re-parenting," has been shown to be very effective in shifting peoples' emotional responses to experiences. It's based on elements of psychodrama and self-hypnosis and variations of it have been used with post-trauma patients to undo the emotional effects of traumatic events.

In all these processes we use our imaginations to re-live the event (or sequence of events) successfully. In some cases, people are invited to remember the beginning of the event and then change the outcome. For people who remember being victims, they "see" the attacker stop, or someone comes in and stops them. For people who remember disasters, it's averted or they're removed from the danger. The goal of these exercises is *not* to change the facts, but to change our emotions so we can choose not to be driven by the emotions associated with these memories. Remember, the subconscious part of us that manages our bodies works on images and feelings, and we're simply giving it another set of images and feelings to work from.

In re-parenting, we re-live our childhoods as if we had the most wonderful parents we can imagine. We see and *feel* ourselves conceived in love and anticipated with delight. We experience being born into loving arms, nursed and nurtured and cuddled and played with. As we "grow up" we see, hear and feel what it was like to be taught with all the patience of unconditional love, guided into finding and developing our gifts, and supported in healthy relationships with our peers and with other adults in the family and community. We discover what it was like to be provided with plenty without being over-burdened with "stuff," taught how to

care for ourselves and others, and being eased out on our own
with all the love and support that we need to be effective adults.

The re-parenting process draws on all our happy memories
(however limited they may seem, at first!) and we add to them
with scenes from movies, books, TV shows, and the lives of others whom we've admired. We do this until it feels as real as any
other memory we have. Then, when it's complete, for most people, a strong enough emotional alternative is in place to make it
possible for them to release any stored upset they may have
around the people they've called "family."

Another method is ancient, indeed. Those who've been
trained by a *shaman* are familiar with the concept of "journeying"
and some may have experience with "soul retrieval." Here, someone who understands the complexities helps us find the places and
people and experiences that had such an emotional impact on our
lives that, effectively, we've left part of ourselves in those times
and places. The idea is to bring those pieces back and restore our
wholeness, our integrity as a being, so we can be fully nourished
and functioning here and now.

In soul retrieval work, people are guided into a past experience or "another world" where they find that they've left "a part
of themselves" wrapped up in some past experience and so are
not fully whole and keep yearning for the part they've left. With
the help of the trained *shaman*, the "missing part" of the person is
retrieved, the soul is completed, the yearning ends, and there is no
more power in the past experience.

Another tool that many hypnotherapists and psychotherapists
now use is "past life therapy." Properly facilitated, an exploration
of experiences from other lifetimes through which a current problem may be more fully understood is a powerful process that can
literally "un-do" the emotional – and often the physical – effects
of past experiences.[42] For example, people who are afraid of the

---

[42] Psychiatrist Brian Weiss was regressing a patient to find childhood distress and heard, instead, about distress in a very different time period,
which he processed as if it were from the patient's current life and resolved

water will typically experience a "past life" in which they drowned, and, realizing it's about a past experience rather than a future possibility, are freed of their fear. People who are afraid of heights or snakes or any number of other things have been known to have similar results.

All of these processes work by creating a state of consciousness, felt as "entering a world (or life)," in which our images and feelings either explain for us or provide a more powerful alternative to what's been going on in our normal, waking lives. Because our subconscious works with images instead of words, the powerful images of a shamanic journey or what's called a "past life regression" can literally replace one set of mental structures with another – resulting in relief from symptoms of all types.

Such shamanic journeys and past life regressions have provided me with powerful insights into my experiences and have also helped un-do patterns in the lives of the people I care about. Realizing that the man I was married to was someone I had experienced hundreds of other kinds of lives with helped me to see why we were drawn together. Being shown in a journey that our relationship was "like a waterfall: everyone around you benefits but the water destroys the rock and the rock breaks up the water into millions of droplets;" helped me to see why it wasn't healthy for us to be married.

Years later, I was working with a man who was "stuck" in adolescent behaviors because of issues resulting from having been abandoned in infancy. One day I was in a shamanic journey and was "handed" him as an infant. Then, over several weeks of inner journeys, my shamanic guides and I nurtured him from that tiny infant through adolescence in the "other world" (without telling him about it in this world). A few months later he met a wonderful woman, gave up a couple addictions, and became a responsible husband and, not long after, father.

---

the issue. He went on to explore the phenomenon and his books and tapes about *Life Before Life* are very helpful, as are similar write-ups by other psychiatrists.

How is it possible for anything I do, by myself, without any-one else knowing, to affect someone else?

From physics and biophysics to consciousness research and the emerging field of psycho-neuro-immunology, the results keep coming back again and again: the feelings we hold about other people affect their brains and bodies and theirs affect ours. Again, the Heartmath Institute and the Institute of Noetic Sciences are compiling the best research in this area, and effective illustrations may be found in the films *What the Bleep Do We Know?* and its sequel, *Further Down the Rabbit Hole,* and also in *The Living Matrix.* Dean Radin's books *Entangled Minds* and *Supernormal* provide detailed accounts, as does the Sounds True book, *Measuring the Immeasurable.*

These experiments demonstrate that we are not these bodies, nor limited by this skin. Whenever we think of someone, their brains and hearts react. When we think positive thoughts, they feel better; when we think harmful thoughts, they feel stressed – *even if they're not aware of it*; their vital signs change. We are not separated!

Back in the 1850s Ralph Waldo Emerson wrote an essay called "History" in which he said, "There is one mind common to all humanity and every man is an inlet and an outlet to the same." He goes on to say that "all history is biography," that what we read in the history of mankind is our own journey. He knew, and wanted his listener/readers to know, too: we are not separated.

Because our experience is a function of what we believe, believing that we or the people we care about are "stuck" in these bodies or in life patterns is what keeps us "stuck." Knowing that consciousness is not limited by our ideas of space and time is the first step to getting "unstuck."

This is the essence of the "miracle" in *A Course in Miracles.* Through our willingness to let go of the old belief, we begin to allow ourselves to function in the greater universe that is outside of our past perceptions. Through our recognition that all that truly exists is this moment, now, we begin to be able to heal ourselves and others of the effects of events that happened "in the past" but exist only as a memory, today.

Remember; the way we influence our bodies, our world, and each other is not by the words we say, but by the meaning of those words: the images and feelings that provide the power that flows *through* the words. So, if we're imagining someone, they feel it – even if they don't know it. (You know this is true: you think of someone and then "bump into them" or get a call or text from them within a few days!) If we're feeling angry thoughts and images toward them, they feel those, too. If we're feeling loving thoughts and images toward them, they not only feel them, they are enhanced by them. And, in most cases, we can count on it that they will respond toward us in the same way we have sent our feelings toward them – just as we respond to the feelings they're having far more than to the words they say. Some teachers have been using this knowledge to make it easier to work with "difficult" students.

This means we have a new kind of responsibility to those around us. Jesus the Christ told his disciples that while Moses' law said not to kill anyone, the truth is that holding angry thoughts against someone else is equally contrary to the Law of Love. Most of us were taught that he said this as a reminder that, if we want to be with (or like) Jesus, we have to be loving in all our thoughts, words, and deeds. And that is true. But it's equally true that to "do no harm" is to not even think thoughts in which others might be harmed (including worrying about what might happen to them). And this is what Jesus, the Master of the Law of Love, was teaching us.

He also taught us to "forgive aught against any," that is, to stop holding anything against anyone for any reason, so we could undo the effects of our past thoughts, words, feelings, and experiences and so begin to experience the "Kingdom" within us and "at hand." Through our willingness to replace anger, hurt, rejection, and resentment with love and light, we "step off the wheel" of *karma*, we "overcome the world," and free ourselves and the others involved of the consequences of the remembered action. We begin to create a new world.

Chapter 6: I'll Make It

Creation

The process of creation is exactly what the opening chapters of the book of Genesis say: first there is emptiness: "all [is] null and void." We get to that emptiness either through training – various martial arts, meditation, and mind-stilling techniques – or through experiencing a shock or insight that is so overwhelming that our normal thought processes are momentarily shut down.

In the emptiness there is a stirring: "the spirit move[s] upon the waters." A breath of insight, a whisper of a possibility, a felt sense of opening, enters into our awareness. If we pay attention and allow it to take its own time, we can follow that subtle movement and experience the next step; we can "let there be light:" the light of inspiration; the dawning of an idea; the clarity of a new vision.

With that vision, we have the beginnings of a framework. We separate what will work from what won't, "light from darkness," and begin to create forms and structures to fill in with the details later. Then the form begins to take on a life of its own, as "the land separated the waters," and as we move with it we see all the new possibilities and new forms emerge, until, finally, the vision is completely manifest – and we rest.

One of the most important things about the creative process is the movement from mind to action to mind to action again. Nothing is fully conceived in the mind and then implemented by the body – everything is partially conceived, partially implemented, and then it's re-conceived and more fully implemented until someone calls it done.

And all along the way, wonderful coincidences and insights and "accidents" move the project forward, almost in spite of our worries and concerns.

A quotation of William H. Murray (that's widely misattributed to Johann Wolfgang von Goethe) describes this process:[43]

...Until one is committed, there is hesitancy, the chance to draw back, always ineffectiveness. Concerning all acts of initiative (and creation), there is one elementary truth the ignorance of which kills countless ideas and splendid plans: that the moment one definitely commits oneself, then providence moves too. A whole stream of events issues from the decision, raising in one's favor all manner of unforeseen incidents, meetings and material assistance, which no man could have dreamt would have come his way. I learned a deep respect for one of Goethe's couplets:

Whatever you can do or dream you can, begin it.

Boldness has genius, power and magic in it![44]

Hard to believe, for sure, but all entrepreneurs and adventurers and founders of nonprofit organizations have discovered the truth of this message!

Mind & Imagination

"Anything the mind can conceive and believe can be achieved," W. Clement Stone learned that from Napoleon Hill and taught it to his apprentices back in the 1950s and '60s.[45] All creative activity begins in the mind, as an idea. Then it moves into the imagination, first as a process, then as an outcome. Then, and only then, can physical activity begin. All the wonders of modern (or ancient) life began in the mind. And all the possibilities for the future begin there, too.

---

[43] William H. Murray *The Scottish Himalayan Expedition* (1951)

[44] The "Goethe couplet" referred to here is from an extremely loose translation of Goethe's *Faust*, lines 214-30, made by John Anster in 1835.

[45] The idea is experessed in most of his books, but his description of having learned it from Hill is in *The Success System That Never Fails*, Napoleon Hill Fndn, 1962, reprinted in 2004.

It's a bit of a cliché, but true: the future belongs first to the dreamers. Back when I was working as a futurist one of our precepts was that "artists and neurotics" are the fore-runners of any emerging societal movement. This is because both groups tend to live, not in the present, but in a set of imagined possibilities for the future.

Then the "movers and shakers" come in and make it happen. Inspired by the possibilities and energized by the opportunity, people like the Wright Brothers, Henry Ford, or Steven Spielberg, or the local PTA put together the resources and bring the dream to life. In one small town I lived in, the members of the American Association of University Women were responsible for virtually every social or environmental improvement project in the community for over a decade. Then, as these women were allowed to join and became active in Rotary and Lions and other service clubs, those groups picked up the baton as "movers and shakers."

Finally, once the new ideas are in place, the rest of us move in and make it our "normal reality," even as we, too often, complain that the dreamers aren't doing enough and the "movers and shakers" are making our lives uncomfortable with all their changes.

Isn't dreaming a waste of time?

Martin Luther King, Jr. "had a dream." He was not alone in having that dream, and in fact, it wasn't even his dream, initially. But he accepted it as his and made it real in his mind in order to "move and shake" the people around him into making that dream a reality in all our experience. His dream was for an America, a world, in which the color of a person's skin would not prevent anyone from fulfilling their potential as a human being. Forty-five years later, this country elected its first non-Caucasian president, and 10 years after that, a woman of African heritage is marrying a prince in line for the British throne.

If no one had imagined that people whose skins were different colors could work and eat and play and study and make a difference together, Colin Powell and Condoleezza Rice would never have been in the US Cabinet (except to clean it), much less served as Secretary of State – and Barack. Obama would never have been a student at Princeton, much less editor of the *Law Review,* and certainly not elected to the U.S. Congress and Presiden-Presidency. If no one had imagined that it was possible to live and work and walk and stay alive on our Moon, we would not have had the space program, with all the fabulous "spin-off" technologies and scientific discoveries that have resulted. If no one had imagined it was possible to live somewhere besides Europe, the Americas would not be what they are today. If no one had imagined it was possible to live where and how you live right now, the building you live in would not exist – nor would the car, the book, the street, the electric light, the music you listen to, or even the clothes you wear.

All the components of our lives started as a dream, a possibility: some vague notion in someone's mind. Then they became "real" in many people's imaginations, and finally, in our experience. So dreaming is by no means a waste of time; in fact, it may be the most important thing we allow ourselves to do!

Projection & Perception

It's easy to see how everything that we have was first born in someone's imagination. But it may be a little more of a stretch to realize that *every* aspect of our experience was first born in our imagination.

As I said before, the sciences of cybernetics and neural psychology have made it clear that we only perceive what we have a mental framework to perceive. And when we encounter something we really can't conceive of, we'll often project our own idea of what *should* be there on top of what is – some magic shows are based on this tendency.

The Buddha said "All that we are is the result of what we have thought." And *A Course in Miracles* goes so far as to say that everything we perceive with our five senses is not what's really there, but is, instead, a projection of what we're expecting to experience. In Lesson 11 the *Course* encourages the student to realize "I'm never upset for the reason I think." This statement is true because, as the *Course* helped the student see in Lesson 7, "I see only the past" (which is why the focus in *this* book is on releasing the past in order to live in the present!).

The principles and discoveries of cybernetics and the neurosciences fully support these ideas. We know that we all have selective hearing: after we've lived with a regular sound for a day or two – a refrigerator or an air conditioner, for example – we no longer "hear" it. It's not that it doesn't enter our hearing system, but that it doesn't enter our awareness. We do the same things with totally unfamiliar sounds and sights: if it doesn't exist in our minds, it doesn't exist "out there." And if we're convinced something must be one way, if our minds are made up – no amount of factual evidence can convince us otherwise. Some politicians have based their entire careers on this phenomenon.

How can someone do that?

One of my favorite examples of how we allow belief to contradict evidence is in Colin Turnbull's book, *The Forest People.* Turnbull, an anthropologist, was documenting the lives, language, and artifacts of a group of African "pygmies" who lived deep in the forest. As often happens, he began to have "an assistant," a young man who was a member of the family group Turnbull was studying and who was learning Turnbull's language and was very interested in all his tools.

One day, the story goes, he invited this young man to travel with him outside of the forest to get some supplies. As they came to the edge of the trees, the vast plains came into view—and, for the first time in his life the young man could see a distance of more than about 50 feet. He was amazed. Off in the distance, a buffalo was grazing. The young man wanted to know what kind of insect that was. Turnbull assured him it was no insect and proceeded to drive to within about 30 feet of the animal without ever losing sight of it. The young man agreed that what was in front of them now was a buffalo, but he held fast to the belief that what they'd been looking at from the edge of the forest was an insect.

It really doesn't matter what's actually in front of us, we won't see what we don't have a framework for, and we *will* see what we expect the world to be like. As Emerson said so long ago, we will only perceive what we're prepared to perceive. The world we see is always what we expect it to be – based on our history and the mental models we've built.

A policeman was trained to enforce the laws and sees the crimes and criminals in the world. A doctor was trained to diagnose and sees symptoms and treatments. A minister sees souls in progress or distress. A realtor or real-estate investor sees properties for sale. A geologist sees stories in rocks and hills. A mother sees families with kids and the parks, stores, schools, and activities that support them – things that, to the rest of us, are invisible, most of the time.

The world we live in is really like those posters that look like a mass of dots until you can see the picture in them.

Or, another way I've come to think of it is as a "green screen", like they use in making movies. A lot of action scenes aren't really filmed on location or even with "real" action. Will Smith battling the giant cockroach in *Men in Black* is really on a ladder in front of a bright, chartreuse green wall. It's a great credit to his acting skill that, when they "filled in" the cockroach around him we experience him struggling in the beast's "arms." Most of the speakers in *The Secret* and *What the Bleep: Further Down the Rabbit Hole* and other interview films are sitting in front of a similar screen that was later filled in with animated graphics.

And, as Virtual Reality – an artificial environment that appears to be real when we wear appropriately programmed sensory devices – becomes available to more folks, more people will use that metaphor for how the world actually works. Just like VR, the world we experience is only as real as the program we're experiencing it through. It is, as the Hindus and Buddhists say, *maya*: a malleable, changing substance that alters as we change our thinking.

Our experience of the world, therefore, has little to do with what may or may not be going on around us. Instead, it's purely a function of our personal "program", our perceptual framework: the beliefs, the memories, the assumptions, and the expectations that we've attached emotions to and *feel* "should be" a particular way. Based on all that, we look around us and "fill in" whatever we're prepared to perceive.

Then we seek out people whose frameworks or "programs" fill things in pretty much the same way as ours, and avoid those whose aren't like ours. That way we can have agreement among the people we associate with that the world looks and acts the way we've decided it does. (Indeed, psychologist Joyce Brothers used to advise people to marry someone whose childhood – hence perceptual framework – was most similar if they wanted a happy life together!) We listen to the talk shows and watch the TV shows and YouTubes that support our perceptions, and staunchly deny the possibility that any other point of view could have any validity.

So our perceptual framework and our projections onto the world around us are continuously reinforced – and our experience is consistent with our beliefs. Thus we construct the box we live in and don't think outside it – until the box collapses around us.

The Mixed-up World We Have

If the world we experience is what our minds "fill in" on a virtual "green screen"[46] based on what we believe and expect the world to be, then *the world will directly reflect whatever is going on in our minds.* This means that if our assumptions, beliefs, ideas, and feelings are conflicting, the world shows up as a mixture of all of them – which is why the world usually seems so illogical and messed up.

Remember, the unconscious mind is very much like a computer. It does what it's told to do: no more, no less. So, when we have mixed emotions or thoughts, we get mixed results in our experience.

If, for example, I grew up in a world of friendly people who enjoy each other's company and help each other out without complaint, and if the songs I learned and the books and TV shows and movies I saw pretty much supported that way of being, that's pretty much what I'll experience for the rest of my life.

---

[46] The plain, lime-green-colored background used in video production when they plan to put other details in later.

But if I grew up in a violent family and community, I can expect to experience the rest of the world pretty much the same way. Or, if I grew up in a family of angry people who lived in a loving, helpful community, the rest of my life will be a mixture of angry family and friends "at home" (including in my job) and loving, helpful friends and neighbors "out there." And, if I grew up in a loving, supportive family in a violent community, that kind of mixture will be my experience – and the basis for whatever actions I take.

We can see this phenomenon occurring over and over in the biographies of famous leaders and celebrities. Martin Luther King, Jr. spoke of growing up in a family where race was a non-issue; respect for individuals as God's children was most important. Mother Teresa spoke of her mother bringing home new "friends" for holidays: poor people she'd picked up off the street. The most powerful story of this type that I know is Anne Miller's *For Your Own Good*. In an analysis of the effects that authoritarian parents have on their children, she describes how Adolf Hitler was raised and how it led to his worldview and later behaviors.

We can also see the process at work in our encounters with people who grew up differently and so experience the world very differently. We see what they do and say in response to the world around them, and we often find ourselves wondering "what planet did you come from?" People who identify as Conservatives and watch Fox TV or listen to their favorite talk-radio shows really can't see that there is another way to look at the world. Progressives and liberals who grew up on the words and actions of Roosevelt, King, and the Kennedys can't comprehend the neo-Conservative point of view. The two groups live, literally, in two different Americas. This fact was made really evident to me on a recent drive through Tex-Arkana – there was only conservative Christian radio, everywhere! No alternatives offered.

And not only are our politics and relationships and expectations about relationships formed in this way, our notions of "pretty," "ugly," "beautiful," "nasty," "amazing," and "normal" – all of our values – are formed the same way. In one household, dark, well-padded furniture with lots of lace doilies and souvenirs of trips taken by family and friends are the norm; in another, straight lines, smooth surfaces, and bright, bold colors is the definition of "clean and comfortable;" in yet another, boxes and piles are strewn around the room and mismatched chairs provide limited seating, defining "home" for those who've grown up that way. People growing up in one environment will tend to have preferences and assumptions that differ widely from those growing up in the other. People moving back and forth between the two are less likely to have definite preferences. In one community, hopping in the car to go a few blocks is the norm; in another, taxicabs and buses do the trick; in another walking or biking is the most common way to get around. People for whom walking or biking is what adults do tend to prefer different kinds of automobiles and are more supportive of mass transit than those who grew up where only kids walk or bike and adults always drive a car.

It's not just an urban-suburban-rural split, either: some farmers buy all they use and sell all they produce and live in modern houses driving new cars; others consume what they produce, make do with older homes and cars, and sell just enough to cover "extras." Some suburban households "get by" on few purchases and others "shop till they drop." Some urbanites make regular trips to museums, libraries, and concerts, while others in the same city don't even know they exist. People in every circumstance consider themselves Liberals, and the same is true for Conservatives – social and fiscal. Similarly for religious orientation.

For most of us, then, the world is a confusing mixture of all these factors plus the American Dream we were taught we could expect to live, mixed with the nightmares of the late '60s and early 2000s, and more than a pinch of romanticized stories about love, warfare, criminal investigations, space exploration, and cowboys mixed in.

For the "X" and "Y" and "millennial" generations, expectations are an even more confusing mixture of all-of-the-above plus a range of ideas about ecology, racial diversity, gender identification, globalization, and political ineffectiveness. As a result, effectively, we have so many possible values and belief systems to choose from that there's no consistent basis on which to design the life and world they desire. – making the labels of "X" and "Y" for recent generations (being the terms used for unknown variables in mathematics) even more appropriate!

But what about genetics? Don't they define our limits?

It's true that a significant factor in how we experience the world is our own biology and inheritance. While there's still a lot of debate over the effects of "nature vs. nurture," we know that each of us is a product of the combination of our genetic and hormonal tendencies, combined with the parenting we received and the society in which we were raised.

Every mother knows that every child is born with unique qualities, different from all others. What we don't know, however, is how many of those differences are the result of the changes in the mother during pregnancy and how many of them are a product of the differences in genes between individual human beings.

The decoding of the DNA molecule, or "genome mapping," was supposed to answer all these questions. Now that it's done, however, what we've learned is that over 99% of our genes are shared with all other human beings, so there can't be too much difference in our genetic heritage! The difference has to be somewhere else in the system.

Bruce Lipton and some other molecular biologists are convinced that the differences between us are the result of the ways the individual cell membranes develop – that what they receive and allow into the cell is what determines how the cell behaves. Lipton's book, *Biology of Belief*, offers a wonderfully clear explanation of this process.

A powerful biological concept called "morphogenetic fields" explains how it is, for example, that individual cells that otherwise are identical change their shape to round over at the tip of the finger instead of continuing to grow straight. Rupert Sheldrake, in his book, *A New Science of Life*, suggests that such fields may guide and direct all human development and behavior; not just the formation of individual bodies.

Such fields are defined by the physiological and cultural norms in which the cells, or people, develop – and, right now, in most communities, there are few consistent norms to guide the formation of individual mind-body systems.

What about free will and personal preferences?

When we choose to say certain things or act in a particular way, we're exercising our will. But how often do we actually choose? How often do we stop to evaluate all of our options and intentionally select the one that fits our current needs and desires most effectively? By contrast, how often do we do what we've always done or what the folks around us have been doing? Too many of us operate on "autopilot" for far too much of our history, with only a very few given the opportunity to wake up. Our words and actions are learned in school, at church or temple, at home, and from our friends; we can do or say only what we've programmed ourselves to say or do.

Our choices are based on the world we perceive and they're made from the unique mixture of processes and programs we've built up over our lifetime. We perceive the world around us and evaluate it and then say something or act in a way that we hope will get us what we want.

Our perceptions, as we've said in earlier chapters, are a function of the mental framework of experiences and emotions that we've built over our lifetimes: we can see only what we're prepared to see. Our evaluations are based on the same framework: we value what is understood and familiar. Our process for selecting what to perceive, what to value, and what to say or do has been developed over the course of our lifetime as the one most likely to bring our perceptions into alignment with our values.

Some of those programs and processes work for us and some don't work. They may generate wonderful experiences or horrible experiences. They often seem to be giving us what we asked for and then don't actually do so. They encourage us to expand our horizons and then will sometimes pull the rug out from under us. Too often, they tell us that our dream costs far more dollars than exist. They constantly tell us we're not okay, not enough, not competent or capable to do what we imagine. Typically, they offer us the moon and the stars even while making it clear there's no way we can have them!

Clearly, the programs we've been living by need to change if we're to change our experience of the world (which is the point of the process in Chapter 4). And, now, for the first time in centuries, in this Great Shift from one era to another, a large number of people have the opportunity and the tools to do so. For the first time in what seems like forever, we can change the programming that has limited us!

The World We Wish For

For hundreds of thousands of years, human beings lived lives based on the cycles of the seasons and of birth-death-and-rebirth. And in some places they still do. In their model of life, we are born, we live as fully as possible, we leave our bodies behind for other beings to use, and we're reborn into a new body.

For the first 200,000+ years humanity's existence was based on the life of the herds that most human populations followed. By far the majority of human beings that ever existed have lived much the same way as the Bushmen of the Kalahari, the "pygmies" of the African forest, the Inuit of Alaska, the dwellers in the Amazonian jungle, and the "aborigines" of Australia do today. They've spent most of their existence in close contact with a variety of plants and animals that provided their food, clothing, tools, and shelter. They studied them and saw the regular cycles of their lives and combined that understanding with their observations of the sun, moon, and stars, climate, and other cycles, along with their own dreams and nightmares. Then they organized these insights in stories and songs to explain the world to their children, and in rituals to help adults remember.[47]

Then, about 26,000 years ago, as the glaciers first began to retreat and the great herds began to die off around the world, a new model was introduced, based on the cycle of cultivated seeds and plants, and an increasingly settled way of life. People gradually

---

[47] While such people may have fewer tools and toys than we do, they are no less intelligent and observant!

identified themselves with smaller areas of land, in which they were born, lived, and were buried.

Their new model of life was found in grain that "dies" as a seed buried in the ground then bursts forth with great, green, vigor and life, then withers and "dies" again as a plant full of seeds that others may eat and re-plant in a cycle of birth – death – life – and rebirth. That model remained in place over most of the world until about 5,000 years ago – and still remains today, in some isolated places. It is the basis of the ancient Sumerian, Chaldean, and Egyptian mythic and religious traditions. It's the basis of the song "John Barleycorn" and the whole Celtic calendar. It's the basis of the "corn dances" of the Hopi, the Zuni, and the Rio Grande pueblos, as well.

Most people that formed villages along rivers and lakes adopted this new model of life, with its stories, songs, and rituals, and their cultures thrived with it for thousands of years. They were (and in some places still are!) gentle and artistic people,[48] sharing their wealth, balancing the dynamics of masculine and feminine energy, loving the earth as a nurturing mother. Their villages had no walls and they made no weapons.

Then, between about 8,000 and 6,000 years ago, a new way of living began to emerge in the Middle East, and spread rapidly along the river valleys.[49] With it, about 4,000 years ago, new idea was introduced: Progress. A small group of human beings began to think that the past is useful only for information and the future is full of potential for a better life.

Where did the idea of Progress come from?

Most scholars relate the idea of linear progress to the linear alphabet, which had been developing as a set of sacred symbols for millennia, but which came into "mainstream" use for record-

---

[48] Excavations of such early villages show no evidence of violent death for hundreds of years, Catal Huyuk in Asia Minor being a notable example.

[49] The details of this process are not widely understood. I've offered one theory in my book *Mary's Power: discovering the divine feminine as the age of empire ends,* published by Portal Center Press.

keeping just about 3200BCE[50] Some scholars tie it to the stories
written in the *Torah*, or Hebrew Bible (the Christian "Old Testament").[51] In these stories we see Abram being guided by a voice
he called *El*, or "Lord," to get up and go somewhere else for a
better life; his grandson Jacob/Israel did likewise; Israel's son Jo-
seph progressed from that way of life to become the 2nd most
important man in Egypt; and brought his brothers and their extended families to live that better life with him. Then his many-
times-great-nephew Moses guided all of their descendants, as one
nation of Israel, out of Egypt toward a better life in the "Promised
Land." Clearly "a better life" is a basic biblical idea.

So it's not too surprising that, following the invention of the
printing press, most of the first generations of Europeans who
were raised reading a Bible at home began revolutions in their
countries. Luther's followers in Germany and Switzerland kicked
out the Roman church and created their own through the
Protestant Reformation. Cromwell's "Puritans" overthrew the
British monarchy and church together – a political order which
didn't last but led, ultimately, to his followers coming to the
Americas. Here their descendants continued the tradition, breaking away from Europe to form the U.S., while others like them
formed all the other nations on the American continents. These in
turn, became democratic republics and contributed to the progres-
sive democratization – disempowering the monarchies of Europe.

Here in the U.S., over the next two centuries, progressing toward a better, brighter future, where all humanity would have
plenty and live in peace became our "Manifest Destiny". Schools,
colleges, and universities were built to ensure that all American
children and adults would share the same values and expectations,
and want to share them with others. Even as these institutions became increasingly secular, the fundamental biblical idea that

---

[50] BCE (before the common era) replaced B.C. (Before Christ) as a more "politically correct" descriptor in the late 1980s. C.E. (common era) replaced
A.D. (*Anno Domini*, or Year of our Lord)
[51] See *The Gifts of the Jews* by Thomas Cahill, Anchor, 1999.

"material and spiritual progress is essential to our well-being" is at the root of all they teach.

In the past hundred years, through Bible-teaching missionaries, the Peace Corps, and the ever-growing "electronic sea," a huge portion of humanity has been introduced to the ideas and possibilities of progress. People all over the world have shifted from being content with living the best possible life within their given circumstances to believing it's necessary to change the circumstances so not only they, but future generations, can have the promised "better life."

As a result, part of the present generations' "programming" is to wish for a better world! A Promised Land! A Kingdom of Heaven on Earth! And this "don't look back; look forward!" world is the world we grew up in. No wonder we're fascinated with end-times!

What's the problem with that?

The dark side of focusing on a better future is that we can't be happy with what we have now. It leads us to believe that what people had in the past is not "good enough," and that what "could be some day" is always more important than what is, today.

As a result, we tend to discount and criticize everything we see as *"passé"* or "out of style" or "old-fashioned." This attitude then leads to a fundamental dissatisfaction with ourselves and our lives, and, if the feelings it generates are repressed long enough, this can lead to an underlying state of consciousness normally diagnosed as "clinical depression" – which some say is the number one illness in the U.S. today, while others say it is among the underlying causes of intense responses to CoViD19 and poor responses to treatment for all kinds of illness.

The World We Can Be Manifesting

Still, we hold ideals of what's possible. They're based in that original idea of "a better, brighter future, where all humanity would have plenty and live in peace." They include things like
  ➢ clear skies with fluffy white clouds and occasional rain,
  ➢ beautiful plants and landscapes,

> ➤ lovely, clean, clear rivers, streams and oceans filled with fish and other helpful forms of life,
> ➤ plenty of food, easily prepared
> ➤ comfortable homes,
> ➤ easy, clean transportation,
> ➤ a sense of community,
> ➤ opportunities to travel,
> ➤ healthy bodies,
> ➤ expanding minds,
> ➤ access to creative arts and expression,
> ➤ meaningful work,
> ➤ supportive families.

This list emerged when I was working as a futurist. Every time I worked with a group to discover their "ideal" future – the one they wanted to work toward – these were the qualities they came up with. Some included villages with minimal automobile use and community centers with lots of educational and recreational resources. Some visions were more urban, with shops and easy, clean, comfortable public transit. Most of them had the "feel" of the 1900s to 1950s small towns in Europe or North America with the addition of modern tools and access to resources.[52] They all had the components listed above.

People want to experience novelty moderated by comfort and effectiveness. They want to be able to learn new things, but in the context of a stable economy and cultural norms that span generations. They want to do things that expand their abilities and contribute to the community, but on their own terms and in their own timeframe. They recognize that things will change with the seasons and with age and experience, but they want that change to be part of a larger context of progress, not just for change's sake.

---

[52] I realize today that my own "perceptual framework" may be "filtering" these peoples' remarks, and it all may be simply my own dreams and wishes being reflected back to me. That could well be the case, and your ideas are, too, dear reader, so this book is simply showing you what you already believe – so now you know what that is. Congratulations! Read on for more!

It's not a model of progress, but it's not a model of cycles, either. It's a new kind of model, one that systems scientists and cyberneticans call a "dynamic equilibrium."

Fortunately, that's a good thing for all of us. Such a way of being can be sustained indefinitely, while our current obsession with constant acquisition and control of novel objects cannot.

If that's the world we dream of, why do we have the mess we're living in today?

It's back to that mixture of thoughts and feelings that form our perceptual framework; they guide all our actions and reactions as we go about doing our work, shoppimg, voting, and otherwise constructing the world we live in.[53]

The fact is, virtually no one who's grown up in the past 100 years actually believes that our dreams can become a reality. We've been taught that our "pipe dreams" have little value, but that "hard work" and "rigorous analysis" and "bigger, smarter machines and weapons" can be counted on.

We've also been taught that it's not okay to have a wonderful life. Many Baby-boomers, believing the words of King and the Kennedys, idolizing Mother Teresa and Gandhi, and raised in a Christian church or Jewish synagogue, were taught that we must sacrifice our own happiness for the good of all, and we have done so. As a result, many of us have given up our dreams so our families, communities, or companies could have what they thought they needed. And in our roles as teachers, politicians, and managers, we have continued to work from those assumptions.

The truth is, however, that *only* our dreams can become our reality. As we saw earlier in this text, what is brought into form existed first as a thought, a dream, an idea. We must first dream something, feeling its form in existence, to experience it.

Sadly, though, because of all the arguments against having our dream world that float around inside us and around us, we tend to think it's "not worth it" to do whatever we've been inspired to do... and that's how dreams die. Like seeds that have

---

[53] The field of "Constructivist Psychology" has developed around this idea.

sprouted and aren't watered, they simply wilt and fall back into the earth.

Making the Dream Real

If we want to convert a thought or dream into material form, we have to be very clear. That is, we can have no mental conflicts. The trick is to eliminate the thoughts, fears, visions, nightmares, songs, sayings, beliefs, opinions, voices, assumptions, and expectations that get in the way of the vision we hold. This is the first step all creative artists must take every time they pick up the tools of their craft.

The next steps move on from that:

2. Get the dream clear . See it, smell it, taste it, hear it, *feel* how it feels to live in the world you've always wanted to live in.

3. Stop listening to all the other kinds of thoughts and voices and songs and sayings that come up as you do so. If you need to you can use an old exercise to "exorcise" those "demons."

    a. Write a few words describing your dream,
    b. Write down all the other kinds of thoughts and words that come up.
    c. When you've run out of the arguments against the dream,
    d. Cross them all off and write your dream again.
    e. Repeat the process until there are no more arguments.

This process will usually be effective for a few months before it needs to be repeated, but, as with the Express-Release-Replace method described in Chapter 4, the second time will be much less intense than the first, and the third much less so than the second, and so forth, until those arguments no longer come up. (*Hooray!*)

To complete the process:

4. Sit quietly (or take a shower or go for a walk or take a long drive) and allow whatever insights and inspirations you're ready to receive. They may be subtle at first, or they may be huge flashes of awareness.

5. Go about your life looking for "synchronicities."[54] These are apparent coincidences, amazingly "weird" or "magical" events that seem to move you in the direction of your dream. Examples:

    a. In James Redfield's book *The Celestine Prophecy*, the first step taking the main character into his adventure was an unrequested, unexpected brochure for a trip to Peru that arrived the day he lost his job and that he found just after an old girl-friend told him he ought to visit that country – then, when he checked it out, there was a last-minute cancellation that let him fly out the next day.

    b. In the movie *The Secret*, Jack Canfield describes having had the inspiration to advertise or get an article about his first book in *The Enquirer* and, a few weeks later, experiencing a woman ask to interview him – then tell him she wrote for *The Enquirer.*

The next step is one many of us miss:

6. *Follow up with action!* We need to take the very next step in front of us; no more. We need only follow up on that one inspiration – and then the next one. As Thomas Edison is often quoted as saying, "genius is 1% inspiration and 99% perspiration".

How do we know what action to take?

In a wonderfully loving conversation called *Emanuel's Book*, Pat Rodegast writes: "you will know the next step from this one. How could it be otherwise?" How freeing! I don't have to know everything now! I don't have to have every detail figured out be-

---

[54] Carl Jung defined these as "apparently unrelated events that are connected by their meaning to the observer." James Redfield made it popular in the 1990s in his *The Celestine Prophecy*, and Rhonda Byrnes et al. in *The Secret* in 2005.

fore I start! Learning this one lesson has made it possible for me to do far more than I ever was able to before.

Emma Curtis Hopkins used to tell her students that all of us have access to all the wisdom and intelligence we need all the time; we just have to stop believing we don't! She said that any time we feel indecision, it's because we've let someone else's ideas become more important than our own, or because we've let our old ideas get in the way of the Good that's always coming toward us.[55] She's reminding us we need to let go of our beliefs that we must be in control or that we must let someone "stronger, smarter, more experienced" show us the way if we are to be effective.

One way to know what is ours to do now is based on a Stanford Business School study of entrepreneurs.[56] The researchers found that the most successful entrepreneurs had a consistent set of criteria: they only did things that took little effort to get started, that they enjoyed, and that they were energized in the process of doing, rather than being tired, drained, or emotionally "worn out." Anything else either didn't need to get done or was best done by someone else. I've translated that into the formula:

Effective = enjoyable + effortless + energizing

A second way is to see what "glows." It sounds strange, to be sure, but, as illustrated in Redfield's *The Celestine Prophecy*, given a choice with all appearances being equal, we can count on having a sense of what direction is ours. It may feel like a "warm glow" in our insides. It may look like a "bright glow" around one of the options. It may "pull" us in one direction or "push" us toward another. All we need to do is relax the body, still the mental chatter, and observe.

When I'm looking for something I need for a project among a set of books or objects, one of them will almost always stand out from the others; it'll "glow" a little more brightly and will be ex-

---

[55] These ideas are expressed in her Lesson 11 in *Scientific Christian Mental Practice,* and explained in the same lesson in my *Unveiling Your Hidden Power.*

[56] *Creativity in Business* by Michael Ray and Rochelle Myers, Main Street Books, 1988.

actly what I need. And when I'm driving, there may be apparently equal options for which way to get where I'm going: I could take this exit off the freeway or another. I could turn at this block or another. So each time I check inside: which way "glows?" Which way "feels" like the best fit in the moment? Which way does my steering wheel "want to" turn? Often I'll find out later that I've missed an accident or heavy traffic or some roadwork by going the way that "glowed" a little more brightly than the other.

Putting these ideas together, the way to know what to do, when, is to:

1. make a list and review the options that are available in this moment, now;

2. "test" each one by *feeling* what it would be like to do it – would it take any effort to start it? Would it be enjoyable to do it? Would I feel energized doing it?

3. if none of the options appears to be more "effortless, enjoyable, and energizing" than the others, simply observe them – check to see if there's any "pull" in your body toward one or another; any "glow" as you look at one or another;

4. begin to take a step, an action, toward the choice you're thinking might work and check again – does this action feel "effortless, enjoyable, energizing?" Does any part of your body feel uncomfortable doing this? If so, consider where the choice came from. Is it a past "program" that you're operating on or is it something real, now?

5. if it feels good (energizing, enjoyable), continue; if not, step back and take another look at the options, repeating the steps above.

Notice that not one of those criteria for choice has anything to do with what someone else told us is the right thing or wrong thing, what we've done in the past, or what we "figure out" will move us toward our goal. In fact, our "figuring-out" mind will generally lead us in a direction that is less than ideal, either physically or emotionally. As Albert Einstein was fond of pointing out, our inner wisdom has access to far more information than our rational, "figuring-out" mind, and always steers us toward what we've set as our most desireable intention.

This means that if we stop letting our old training, "programming," and fears get in the way, we can allow the wisdom that's available to all of us, always, begin to inform us. Then we can always know when and how to speak or act without concern or indecision. Now that's true freedom!

So how do I set an intention, or even know what intention to set?

Setting intentions involves the same decision-making process as starting to act. It's just that the options are inside us, rather than in the world around us.

Remember all the experiences in your past when you felt *really* good, satisfied, glad to be alive, excited, jubilant, fulfilled. Remember the place, the people, the temperature, the events leading up to that moment, the things you were doing, saying, and thinking;

1. write each one of these experiences down, in as much detail as you can remember;
2. look over all those times and find what is repeated in many of them – was it the same people? The same kind of activity? The same temperature? The same light? Was it when you were winning something? Creating something?
3. list all the qualities, people, and characteristics that were present in these experiences;
4. now review the list and add any more qualities, people, characteristics, that you now enjoy, that you've discovered, or think could make you feel *really* good now or in the near future.

This is the set of qualities and the kind of people you would like to have in your life forever. These are the main components of your "dream world," your "heaven," your "paradise." This list is your *real* intentions for your life – regardless of what your childhood "programming" or people around you say they "should" be.

With this in mind, you can do the steps for making a choice that we used above: check with your body: does this new intention *feel* energizing, enjoyable, effortless? If so, you're more likely to be on target than with any other deciding factor.

How do dreams and ideals become a world?

Thousands of people over the centuries have discovered that clarifying our dreams and ideals means that, even before we start to make them real in the world around us, we'll begin to have more and more experiences in which we feel really good. Often, they'll happen in places and doing things we never could have imagined or "figured out" on our own.

In Wallace Wattles' *The Science of Getting Rich*, he says that the universe is structured to fulfill the nature of all beings: that as seeds have within them and around them all that they need to become forests, so we have all that we need within us and around us to develop our gifts and talents fully – and that what we most enjoy in life is the clearest sign of our gifts and talents.[57]

His book was what turned Rhonda Byrnes' life around and led to her production of *The Secret* and all the videos and books associated with it. She also drew heavily on the teachings of Esther and Jerry Hicks, whose work on "the Law of Attraction" teaches us that we receive from the universe the energy that we put out into it, so if we want to feel good about our lives in the future, we need to feel good about them now.[58]

So, when we begin to know what our ideal world looks like, feels like, tastes like, smells like, and sounds like, and when we begin to enjoy whatever even comes close to that ideal, then we actually draw from the universe around us more of the same.

We draw things into our lives from the universe?

Yes, I know, this sounds like *The Twilight Zone*. But literally thousands of people over thousands of years have been practicing

---

[57] *The Science of Getting Rich* is available in its original form from a number of publishers—my "translation" of it is *The (New) Science of Getting Rich* published by Beyond Words/Simon & Schuster in 2008.

[58] *The Law of Attraction* by Esther and Jerry Hicks, Abraham-Hicks Publications, 2006.

this "magic formula," this "alchemy" with brilliant results. People ranging from Arthur's Merlin to Isaac Newton, from Queen Elizabeth I to Napoleon Hill and from Andrew Carnegie to Tony Robbins have built their lives, their fortunes, and their worlds, using these principles.

Three things are happening as you do this process.

1. First, you're telling your body-mind system which of the many memories and inputs to pay attention to.
2. As you do so, it begins to see the world differently;
3. Things that have been there all along are suddenly visible and useful.

It's really an amazing thing to observe!

Here's an example that you *don't* want to emulate. For a few years, I did a form of community development work called "Neighborhood Watch." It was my job to train urban residents to identify possible threats on their block and to work together to be safer. (Some of you are already seeing where I'm going here!) I spent several hours each month in meetings with police personnel and occasionally was given rides in police cars to or from those meetings. It was my job to know the neighborhood, its residents, and its "characters;" it was their job to recognize and stop any activity that was against the law or endangered anyone. Invariably, as we were driving along, the police personnel would see people in the neighborhood that were either endangered, endangering someone else, or breaking the law. I stopped doing that work soon after my supervisor, and then a month later I, came home to find a burglar in the house – an event that's never happened before or since, and I've lived in a lot of tough neighborhoods.

That story is just one small example of how we experience what we focus on. I'm guessing that, if you look back over your life experiences, you could find a few more – hopefully more positive ones.

What else is happening?

The second thing we're doing as we clarify the qualities of our "ideal dream world" is to give ourselves a clear basis on which to make our choices. As outlined in the process defined above, our intentions are the primary criteria we use when we decide to act. By stating them, we've begun to rearrange our perceptual framework and our decision-making apparatus. We're more likely to act according to stated intentions and to focus on all the ways (however small or large they may be) that these qualities and experiences are showing up in our lives, instead of all the ways we don't have them. Then, as we act in alignment with our happiest, most satisfying experiences, we're doing things that feel better and we're bringing forth more of those kinds of things through our actions.

A third thing happens as we clarify our intentions, allow ourselves to enjoy what we're experiencing, and choose in alignment with that enjoyment. We're "reprogramming" the part of our unconscious mind that's working around us as well as within us to identify and move us toward what will fulfill us.

As I said before, the unconscious mind is very much like a computer. It does what it's told to do: no more, no less. That's why when we have mixed emotions or thoughts we get mixed results in our experience.

Really? My mind changes the world around me?

One way to understand how our minds affect the world around us is to look at a remarkable experiment performed at Princeton University. For years, computer operators have played games with printouts and screens, using a program called a Random Number Generator. Very simply, this program prints, or shows on a screen, a series of 1s and 0s that have no pattern to them—they're almost totally random. The computer might be displaying a set of 1s and 0s that might look something like the grid in the film *The Matrix*:

```
10111011010010000100101000101100110101111010001010
01101010010111010010111001010001001010100000101001
00111011101101001000010010100010111011010111010001
01001100100001010000100111111000101011101101101100
```

The often-bored computer operator would look at the screen or printout and decide to see something different: maybe a string of 12 1s or 20 0s and maybe even more than one such string. After a while, some would get so good they could "make" squares and other shapes with the 1s and 0s that the computer was generating – without ever touching the computer!

This process is so well documented among computer folks that Princeton got a grant to see what would happen if a bunch of computers were connected, each with its own Random Number Generator. They set up 85 computers in various places around the world and through the internet connected one printer to all of them in the lab at Princeton. They wondered if what was going on in the world would affect the combined sequences the way what a computer operator could for a single one.

It did, in a huge way, on September 11, 2001, when the whole world was in shock as they watched the World Trade Center towers collapse under the impact of a jet airliner. The nice little wiggly line that usually went across the middle of the printout in the lab at Princeton began to change on the morning of the 10th, getting further and further away from "normal," then it sank a little below its norm overnight, began to rise again on the morning of the 11th, and went off the scale an hour or so later, when California woke up. The line dipped down, but still way above normal, for another day, then after a couple days back in its normal pattern. It dipped well below normal again during the "minutes of silence" that President Bush called the world to observe at noon that Friday.[59]

What's 9/11 got to do with how our minds can change the world?

Well, if our thoughts and emotions can change the printout on a computer, then imagine what else they might be doing!

---

[59] You can see the whole thing—and a number of other events—by doing a search for The Global Consciousness Project on the internet or going to www.noosphere.princeton.edu. Needless to say they were given a lot more money and have since set up a lot more computers around the world, and there continue to be remarkable results. A radio show, Coast-to-Coast AM, has done some interesting experiments with the system, too.

Remember, everything in the world is made up of the same stuff that computers operate on – electrons and smaller subatomic processes. If the electrical and electronic systems of computers respond directly to what we're feeling, then everything else must respond, too!

We all knew, that morning, that the world was changed for good. Most of us thought it was the beginning of a world defined by terrorist acts. It may be, however, that years from now historians will see this little computer experiment as the most important event – the beginning of the next stage in history, and certainly of a new generation – for because of it, we can no longer pretend that we're separated from each other, or from the world of things. Because of this computer printout we can *see* that our minds affect the world around us – even before we're all aware of it!

So the choices we made on 9/11/01 and the days that followed not only affected our nation and our lives. They affected the direction the world has taken ever since.

Chapter 7: Some Day

After hearing all those ads and news stories about how the future was going to be so much better, the Baby-boomers had to learn the hard way that "progress" isn't all we were led to believe it would be. Sadly, though, we still think that the past is "passé" and that this moment, now, is barely tolerable. Most of us, and many of our children, are still hoping that "some day" things will be better.

Most current forecasts and prophecies, however, do not concur. From Christians to Mayans, Hopis to aboriginal Australians, environmentalists to economists, we're being given a very different message. We're being told that this world, which has seemed so permanent, so fixed, so stable, is beginning to go through massive changes, some disastrous, which will affect us profoundly, and could even wipe humanity out.[60] More disturbingly, many of those forecasts and prophecies are telling us that we're coming to the end of the world as we know it!

How can the world end?

This world, we're told in many spiritual teachings, is not what God created. In modern Western culture, most of us have had to wrestle with the very idea of a Creator. The Intelligent Design vs. Evolution debate is a vivid indicator of our conflicting thoughts

---

[60] For a more detailed description of these prophecies and forecasts, see *Maya Cosmogenesis 2012: The True Meaning of the Maya Calendar End-Date* by John Major Jenkins and Terence McKenna or *Apocolypse 2012: the ticking of the end-time clock* by John Claeys or my summary *Beyond 2012. Hope for a New World* on YouTube. Although the dating is far less specific than these title suggest, the basic principle — that this is a time when one age is ending and another, with very different qualities is beginning — is well established.

on the subject – and as someone trained in the sciences, I'm fully aware of the issue! But across the world traditions, from Taoism to Islam, Buddhism to Wicca, Shamanism to the Judeo-Christian tradition, there is agreement on one thing: the Source of All That Is is an intelligent, creative process with a fundamentally loving quality. Whatever name anyone gives it (remember, the Power is not in the letters of a word!) the Creative Source of All That Is can be counted on to continue to expand and create and develop in more and more mutually supportive ways – and *only* in those ways.

What's been created, therefore, must be intelligent and loving – and must continue to be even more so. It can't be otherwise.

This means, they tell us, that this world we experience is what *we've* made, based on our belief that we were separate from all that indefinable Source is; that we are separate from the divine, absolute Reality of loving intelligence. The world we experience every day is what the Hindus and Buddhists call *maya*, which means changeable, malleable, not eternal – while what our Source, being eternal, has created must be eternal. This world, the great teachers through the ages have told us, is something we've made up because we didn't know we could experience the true Reality. And, they've told us, all we need to do is wake up if we want to experience the Reality that God created, to enjoy what Jesus called "The Kingdom of Heaven."

This understanding is totally aligned with what we've said so far in this book, we've seen the truth of the teaching: that the world we've been experiencing, individually and collectively, is a function of our perceptual framework. It's not Reality; not a permanent eternal creation.

That means it can end, and a new world can replace it. It can happen instantaneously or it can take generations. Our choice.

What does it mean when people say "end of the world?"

Happily "the world," it's clear from all the different cultures that talk about it, does *not* mean the planet Earth or the universe of stars and planets. "The world," as they use the term, means the *experience* of people, places, things, and emotions that we're accustomed to.

The word in the Bible that's usually translated as "world" actually means "eon" or "era." And the word that is usually translated as "end" actually means "fulfillment," as in "the living end!" The same applies to the translations of other languages we've been working with, including the Mayan and the Hopi, who are explicit that they're referring to eras.

So what's really meant by "the end of the world," is that one way of living, one set of assumptions about what works and doesn't work in life, has run its course and is about to be replaced by another. Hooray!

All the things that we take for granted will be shaken up. All our values and priorities will be realigned. The way we live will be very different. Yippee!

And, according to all the prophecies and forecasts, this is not the first time it's happened. Some say this is the fourth or fifth time humanity has been through this kind of process.[61]

Sadly, though, they also say that we've waited so long to pay attention to this process that, like most things that are dealt with at the last minute, "it ain't gonna be pretty." And, with CoViD19, political unrest, and huge storms and droughts, we're beginning to get a sense of what that means.

What are these prophecies?

Many prophecies, from all over the world, have tried to tell us that our basic assumptions about the nature of the universe aren't accurate and need to change. They've tried to help us break through our culture's insistence that this malleable world of matter is fixed and real so we could move on to the next "world," or stage in our development.

---

[61] The movie, *The Sixth Sun*, explains this idea from many cultural viewpoints.

A visionary figure that Christians call Our Lady tried to help us wake up at Fatima in the 1930s and at Medjugorje in the 1980s and '90s. She told those who could see her (three children in both places) to pray for peace and to tell the world to pray for peace. She then gave specific examples of the kinds of things we might experience if we continue to choose to act from greed and violence rather than focus on loving each other and the divine.

The Hopi elders, following their ancient story that the day would come when the Hopi (which means "people of peace") would go to the "mica tower" on the shore of the Eastern Sea, actually went to the United Nations to speak to the elders of the nations of the world and tell them they must change their ways to avert a catastrophic ending to this world. The story says they would "knock 4 times," and the elders went 3 times. The 1st time they were ignored completely. The 2nd time was in 1992, when the U.N. Conference on the Earth was scheduled in Brazil, and they, along with many other indigenous peoples who camped outside the hotel, were able to talk with some U.N. officials. The 3rd time, after the world had begun to realize that indigenous elders had something worth listening to, they spoke to the General Assembly, though only a few attended.

They told the leaders of the world their story: how the Hopi had been entrusted with keeping the western hemisphere in balance until their true white brother arrived and the Great Spirit's hopes for mankind were fulfilled. They said how important it was to choose away from war and greed and to begin to live in harmony with Nature.[62]

That was over a decade ago. Clearly, we have not listened.

The Mayan story is that what they call this past Long Count (5135 years) has been one in which humanity has been driven by overwhelming materialism and hunger for power; that it was a necessary stage in humanity's development, but that, with the end of the current cycle, these ways of living would be over.

---

[62] Willie Whitefeather's short film *Hope* illustrates their message beautifully.

It's interesting to note that the beginning of the Mayan Long Count, August 11, 3114 BCE, is also, really, the beginning of what we call Western Civilization. Among other things:

> ➤ Empires and written history began in the fertile crescent of the Middle East about 3100 BCE;
>
> ➤ Core samples say solar flare activity increased and the Sahara was suddenly transformed from greenbelt to desert about 3100 BCE so lots of people moved into the Nile valley, leading to the formation of the first city-states;
>
> ➤ Hindus, Jains, and Buddhists agree that we're completing a several-thousand year old cycle. The ancient Hindu tradition says that Krishna died and the current, Degenerate Age, began in 3102 BCE and ended, like the Mayan calendar, when the sunrise returned to its "home" in the dark rift at the center of the galaxy, on or about December, 2012.

Astronomy plays a role here. Ancient Chaldean and Babylonian astronomers documented a phenomenon we call Precession, in which the sun appears to rise in different sectors of the sky over the course of a 26,000 year cycle. The signs of the Zodiac that we know today, plus one that we no longer use, divide that cycle into 13 sectors of 2000 years.[63] According to their calendar, Moses lived when the Age of Taurus, the Bull (or golden calf) was shifting into the Age of Aries, the Goat (or sacrificial lamb). Jesus lived when the Age of Aries was shifting into the Age of Pisces, the Fish. Right now the Age of Pisces is shifting into the Age of Aquarius, the Water-bearer (been carrying your bottle of water around lately?), and the current 26,000 year cycle is coming to an end in the early years of this century.

About 75,000 years ago, almost three 26,000-year precessions ago, Toba, the Sumatran caldera, blew up and the ash-cloud lowered earth's temperature 5 to 10°C (45 -50°F) in 10 years – which

---

[63] The Chaldeans and Babylonians had a 13th sign that was lost over the centuries as empires shifted from a lunar to a solar year. As a result, our signs of the Zodiac occur at different times from the ones they studied.

some say started the last ice age. Interestingly, many native stories say that before the world ended in water (the Flood), one ended in mud (melting glaciers?), and the one before that ended in ice.

Some ancient traditions say that this world, this eon, ends in fire. The Hopi and some other Native Americans connect it to the "gourd of ashes," which is their name for the atom bomb. Several say that the end will start with wars in the Middle East, the land of the ancient Babylonians and the place where Western Civilization began. This means that the birthplace of urban life and empires may become the deathbed for them, as well.

They tell us that when that is about to happen, we will see signs: the sky will turn red; stars will shift and seem to cry; people in the cities will get sick and fight for food.

One Native American elder, Lee Brown, spoke about these times to a gathering of native leaders from around the continent in Alaska in 1996. Among other things, he shared prophecies from the elders of many tribes and nations in the Americas, and the following guidelines:

...they said at this time you're going to see that things will speed up, that people on the earth will move faster and faster. Grandchildren will not have time for grandparents. Parents will not have time for children. It will seem like time is going faster and faster. The elders advised us that as things speed up, you yourself should slow down. The faster things go, the slower you go.

Go on the mountains and make a place for yourself. Put some things there that you can survive with... [64]

His description of our current world experience fits almost too well.

That's what the prophecies say, but what about the science?

Several of the sciences support the essence, if not all the details, of these prophetic traditions.

---

64 Lee Brown on the American Indian Prophecies, 1996 Continental Indigenous Council, Tanana Valley Fairgrounds Fairbanks, Alaska

Most prophecies over the past several thousand years have said that those who live by greed, competition, and discord will have to struggle as a result. Analyzing them from a psychological perspective, that makes sense:

> ➤ someone who believes the world is a fearful place will operate in fear;
> ➤ operating in fear involves either avoiding possible dangers by limiting one's activities or attempting to control everything so it can't endanger one;
> ➤ both limiting oneself and trying to control others are hard on both body and soul – the one makes it hard to develop and learn and the other takes a lot of time, energy, and attention;
> ➤ lack of development and excess energy use weaken the mind and body over time;
> ➤ the weakened mind-body system gets sick or makes choices that are damaging.

From an ecological perspective, we can see that accumulating stuff or controlling people changes the environment one lives in: the stuff needs to be cared for and protected and the people are not to be counted on for support. So not only is the fearful path damaging to the mind-body system, it creates an environment that's no longer supportive.

Taking the ecological view still further, the act of producing and accumulating stuff has an impact on the larger environment that reduces available resources and fills it with garbage, so leaves it weaker and less able to support the people in it. So a community or culture of accumulators ultimately runs out of resources to accumulate. This is what happened in places like Lebanon, which once boasted great forests of cedars, or the Gobi desert, which was also once a great forest. It's the essence of Donella Meadows' books *The Limits to Growth* and *Beyond the Limits,* and is beautifully described by Daniel Quinn in his award-winning novel, *Ishmael.*

Today we see global changes ranging from melting polar ice caps to increased landslides and volcanic activity and changing weather patterns, to economic hardship resulting from failed crops or transportation systems. Some forecasts say that a continued dependence on fossil fuel leads to more of the same results.

These are clear examples of how our attitudes and assumptions have led to actions that are changing how the Earth's systems function. Driving cars and using lawn mowers and boats with internal combustion engines, burning coal and oil and natural gas in factories and power plants to make and power electric heaters and air conditioners in buildings hundreds of miles away have an impact. But both add about as much CO_2 to the atmosphere in a decade as a single volcano does in a day.

Cutting down large areas of trees also changes the rainfall patterns across a region, and reduces the amount of oxygen being produced and CO_2 being stored by the trees that have been removed from the system. The crop cycles and flood/erosion patterns are changed as well – leading to reduced food supplies and increased desertification, all for the sake of a few peoples' short-term financial gain. Massive use of concrete and asphalt, combined with large numbers of automobiles and air conditioners typically raise the temperature in an urban setting by as much as 20°F – which then affects the rain and snowfall patterns in that area, and may set up air currents that change other regions' weather patterns.

None of these actions are necessary; all of them are based on faulty assumptions about how the earth's systems work, justifying immediate profit over long-term gains. Selective harvesting of trees has been proven to be both economically and ecologically more effective than clear-cutting, for all tree species. The Eco-Forestry Institute and other sustainable forestry organizations have demonstrated many times that taking out 20% of trees in a forest each year usually results in more timber after 5 harvests than at the beginning. Well-designed urban areas that include effective mass transit with substantial tree canopies to shade buildings and streets and are oriented to maximize natural airflows don't have to become "heat pockets."

Both approaches depend on cooperation and lack of greed among the people in the region to be implemented. Over and over, they've been proven to be most effective for both short term and long term sustainability. But in a culture based on the assumption that the world is dangerous and which encourages fear and greed, short-term gain outweighs long-term benefits, so cooperative solutions are rarely implemented—and urban areas and forests are both rapidly becoming deserts, as they have throughout this past Long Count "world" of this Empire Culture in which we live.

The Beginning of the Next World

If we look at all the prophecies and forecasts associated with this period in human history, we see a common thread that can be stated as:

Now is the time for all of humanity to begin to live the way that a few spiritual teachers and avatars have been showing us for centuries.

If we're just moving from one age to another, what does the next age look like?

The Mayans tell us that:

> ➤ As we approach the shift, time seems to be both moving faster than ever and not moving at all;
> ➤ We begin to live in the now; the Present moment, no longer governed by the clock.
> ➤ As we do so, we experience more "flow" of unity, letting go of the ego sense of duality, so in 2011, the dominance of the dual mind (good/bad; dark/light; right/wrong) withers.
> ➤ In Oct 2011, the sun entered the "Universal Awareness."... This is when some of us can fully understand the cosmic plan and, in our overflowing gratitude, recognize our own divinity, and as we do so there will be no separation.
> ➤ In 2012 the elders of the past returned to make a communication between the heart of humanity and the heart of the earth...

> It's the beginning of a new era of peace, harmony, love, and union…

The new world, or era, is one in which technology will be based in spirit and biology; life will be enhanced for all beings; humanity will take on new forms.

In 1992, Hopi elder Dan Evalema told the General Assembly of the U.N.,

> *…even if there are only one, two, or three of the true Hopi who remain holding fast to the last ancient teaching and instructions the Great Spirit, Massau'u will appear before all, and our would will be saved. The three will lay out a new life plan which leads to everlasting life and peace. The earth will become new as it was from the beginning. Flowers will bloom again, wild game will return to barren lands, and there will be abundance of food for all. Those who are saved will share everything equally and they all will recognize Great Spirit and speak one language.*

Ken Carey, in his book *Vision*, confirms this image of the world we are about to experience. He describes a world where spiritual and mental awareness is so powerful that people can change their bodies at will and adapt to very different living environments.

From John's *Revelation* through the Hindu *Vedas* the story is essentially the same. There's a major shift in the way the world works, made more difficult if we don't prepare for it, then an extended period of peace, harmony, cooperation, and emphasis on spiritual development.

Across the prophecies, once we get through the mess we've created by not paying attention, it looks like we're headed into something pretty wonderful for some people:

> The "sixth age" or "fifth world"
> The "Age of Aquarius"
> The "Age of Light"
> The "Aeon of Horus"
> A "blend of all cultures and colors"
> A global humanity focused on spirituality, healing, wholeness

> ➤ A "new heaven" in a "new earth"

So be it.

Chapter 8: You Love Me

"I've loved you with an unending love... "[65]

One of the great myths of this world is that each of us is an isolated individual, struggling in a hostile environment to survive and make a life for ourselves and our families. Our whole culture is designed around the "rugged individual," the great hero, fighting his way through a world of darkness and despair to find and hold onto a tiny shred of light and hope.

Some say that the belief that we are separate and isolated and that the world is dangerous begins with the traumatic experience of being born – especially being born in a hospital setting with bright lights and sharp instruments and being put in a crib away from sound of the heartbeat and breathing and voice that defined our home for so many months.

With all of that, it seems totally reasonable to feel separate and alone.

In fact, however, nothing could be further from the Truth! Even though an essay by Ralph Waldo Emerson, called "Self Reliance" is often pointed to as justification for this belief, he very clearly did not believe we are, or should act as isolated beings. His very first set of essays, on "Nature" stated, almost two hundred years ago,

Spirit, that is, the Supreme Being, does not build up nature around us, but puts it forth through us... Man has access to the entire mind of the Creator, is himself the creator in the finite.

And, as was cited above, his essay "History" starts with the statement that "there is one mind common to all humanity and every man is an inlet and outlet to the same." Clearly he didn't be-

---

[65] From a poem by Rabindranath Tagore, in which God speaks to mankind.

lieve we're isolated beings. The "self" in "Self-Reliance" is our inner Self, which, he said, we share with all Creation!

But all our schools, our media, our dramas, have convinced us this is not so. They've encouraged us to believe that we can't expect others to care about us or to work with us or for our well-being. They've told us that to cooperate is to give up something precious – our individuality – and that our success is a function of our competitiveness. And because we've believed it, we've experienced it.

We've also been convinced that we must "be good" to be loved, and "do good" to be granted nourishment and support. More than that, they tell us daily that we're never "good enough." And again, our experiences have reinforced and supported our beliefs.

The first lesson of the great New Thought teacher, Emma Curtis Hopkins[66] has one consistent theme: God (by whatever name we use) is all that exists and God is Good; therefore all that exists is Good, and, if we exist, then we must also be fundamentally Good.[67] Interestingly, some linguists suggest that the English word God derives from the German word for good.

If we consider what modern physics is telling us about how the universe works at the most fundamental level, Hopkins' assertion that Good, or God, is all that is, makes sense. The sciences tell us that there's no "old man in the sky" writing down all the good and bad things we've done in a great Book of Judgment. There's just an unfolding process of development, in an all-pervading field of order: Good. We can call it Light or Life or Peace or Harmony or Order or Balance, or Love, or any other name that we consider good—because it's all One.

---

[66] Hopkins is called the "teacher of teachers" because her students included all the founders of the various New Thought churches: Fillmore, Holmes, Brooks, Hiltz, and more.

[67] This concept is present in all the versions of her 12 lessons. These words are from my "translation" of her work: *Unveiling Your Hidden Power: Emma Curtis Hopkins' metaphysics for the 21st Century,* WiseWoman Press, 2006.

And only our belief that we're separate from that One – our ideas about the world being filled with "others" we must fear – lead us to see and experience it as we do. As Hopkins puts it in her second lesson, "matter is all the obstruction there is; it is the result of our belief that we are separate from our Good." In this she helps us see that when we focus on matter and how it works, we are limited, but when we focus on the infinite Source of all, then those limitations fall away.

How do we know it's all good?

In his introduction to *The Power of Now* Eckart Tolle tells us that when he was at the end of his emotional rope, when he knew that tomorrow he must necessarily die, he collapsed in the dark; then woke up seeing the world a whole new way – everything glowed; everyone was extending themselves to everyone around them; and for several months, he had no experience of need or want; all was provided without any effort on his part.

Shamans, saints, and mystics all tell similar stories: when they let go of their assumptions about the world and focus their attention on the Light, everything is taken care of.

A few teachers have said much the same. Jesus said not to worry about food or clothing because God will make sure we're royally supplied—"even Solomon in all his glory was not so beautifully dressed!" Ralph Waldo Emerson, deliberately reaching out to the unchurched population of the 19th century U.S., said (I'm paraphrasing from his essays "Nature" and "Spiritual Laws" here) that if we would simply accept our true Self, we would outshine all the beauty that Nature has to offer and Nature, herself, would respond to our every need.

If we stop to think, we realize that most of us, today, have far more things and live far more comfortably than royalty did, even 200 years ago. A palace is really an apartment house or hotel (as many former palaces are being used today); a bunch of servants can't do more than our modern conveniences supply for us; most of us have far more clothes than we could wear in a month; and even the oldest, cheapest car can go much further and faster than a horse—and far more comfortably! That's not even addressing our telephones, televisions, and computers!

So if we look back over our lives, most of us have had it pretty good. In fact, most of us have never been hungry (except when we were on a diet), never been without a warm, dry, place to sleep (except when we went camping), and have never not been able to do pretty much whatever we set our minds to do – unless we chose otherwise out of the "have to" list in Chapter Two..

Even if we look back through history, most human beings have had everything we needed in each 'now' moment, to be okay (as defined by people in that time and place) in that moment.

So, yes, we can know that life is Good.

What about all those who don't have what they need?

We're used to thinking of people who live in grass or mud huts in small villages as "poor." But that's looking through our own perceptual frameworks. Studies have shown that those who follow the "old ways" of such cultures only work about 4 hours a day, 6 days a week to meet all their needs, comfortably.[68] They spend their free time making beautiful things and dancing and singing and exploring their inner and outer worlds, and many of them live far longer than most of us in western culture! So clearly they have all they need.

It's true that there are starving children and lost refugees and people dying of disease and accidents, and far too many other truly sad and often horrible experiences for some people. And that's not okay. The actuality is, however, (in spite of what the media would have us believe) that those are a very tiny fraction of humanity – even CoViD19's death rate is less than 3% of those infected. And, according to the UN and other sources they're rapidly decreasing, worldwide. Moreover, looking back on such times, horrible as they were, people have often said that those experiences were the "wake up call" they needed to change their way of thinking and living. Then there's the fact that, in many cases –

---

[68] A recent film called *Babies* illustrates this beautifully.

though by no means all – the "problems" they're having aren't nearly as distressing for those going through them as they are for those of us watching from our own perspective.

I say all that as someone who has been a single mom and the daughter of a single mom, who grew up in the inner city, has lived out of a car for lack of a home, has worked multiple jobs to support my kids, has spent two decades working as a minister in rural communities, gave up a small fortune by selling houses I helped rehab to low-income families, has been bedridden with an unknown ailment for months, and has since helped create a nonprofit providing transitional housing for otherwise homeless men and women.

I say that as the grandchild of missionaries—on both sides of the family. They all went with high hopes of changing the world. And they all came home understanding that the "awful conditions" they'd gone over to reverse weren't nearly as awful as they'd been led to expect – that, in fact, much of what they'd seen were totally logical ways to deal with the climate and culture they were in. Yes, there were some things that could make life easier or create more and healthier opportunities, and my grandparents were able to help; but it made no sense to try to impose American industrial values on village farmers in other countries.

In fact, my grandparents learned that often the "helper" is the one who needs help. They realized that some of their own ideas about the world were not as useful as those of the people they were there for – and might in fact cause more problems for those people. And more, they all came home with a new respect for the ways that "the Good Lord does provide" – for everyone.

Everyone? The Creative Source provides for everyone? The whole universe?

Believe it or not – and you wouldn't have to ask the question if you did believe it – it's becoming more and more clear that we're all provided with as much as we accept, all the time.

A few years ago I was asked to "translate" (interpret for modern readers) a book written at the end of the 19th century called *The Science of Getting Rich* (I've referred to it several times in this book; it's what inspired Rhonda Byrnes to create *The Secret*). While I truly enjoy the process of making material that was written in Victorian rhetoric accessible to the TV-and-internet generations, I wasn't sure I wanted to do a book with that title. (In fact, all the way through the process I kept offering the publishers alternative titles!) But I accepted the job when I started to read the book. Nowhere had I seen it stated so clearly:

No one is kept in poverty by limits in the supply of riches; there's more than enough for all. ...In truth, the visible supply is practically inexhaustible, and the invisible supply really is inexhaustible...

Nature is an unlimited storehouse of riches; the supply will never run short...

The formless substance responds to the needs of mankind; it will not let humanity be without any good thing...

Nature exists for the advancement of life, and its primary impulse is the increase of life. Because of this, everything that can possibly enhance life is bountifully provided.[69]

He goes on to say that the only reason any individual doesn't experience this total support and advancement is because they haven't learned how to think and act in a way that allows it.

I was also asked to translate some of the works of Ralph Waldo Emerson. In the process I discovered that, about fifty years earlier, in his essay "Nature," Emerson encouraged us to look at the incredible abundance of seeds produced by a tree to help us understand how truly abundant Nature really is. If one tree, without any effort or strain, simply by being a tree, can produce so much, how much more is available to us?

Jesus the Christ and Gautama the Buddha, like the great teachers of all traditions, encouraged us to stop worrying about what we might *not* have in the future and start appreciating all that we *do* have, now.

---

[69] *The NEW Science of Getting Rich*, Wallace D. Wattles, edited by Ruth L. Miller, Beyond Words/Atria, 2007.

Our Place in the Quantum Uni-Verse

The word Universe comes from the Latin, meaning "one song" or "one turning." It is usually used as a synonym for "whole," "entire," or "all that exists."

In her remarkable exploration of quantum possibility, *Quantum Self*, Danah Zohar says that if we really understand the ways subatomic quanta work, we'd realize that we only exist *in relationship to others*. That is, who I am is a function of my interactions with all of you, and vice versa. She came to this understanding while pregnant. (Makes me wonder what would have happened if more physicists had been able to be pregnant sooner!) She had long been well aware of the ways subatomic matter and energy behaved in relationship, but her own sense of self changed as she became aware of the life that was developing within her. She came to realize that not only was her body changing, but her mind, her emotions, and her expectations of others were changing as well: she was becoming a different person because of her relationship to this new being. She realized then that all form is just that.

We are all a mixture of matter and energy, and energy is present everywhere across space and time. So everything that exists, including us, is a mixture of energy-fields that overlap with other fields, each with their own tendencies, and all are constantly being modified by those overlaps. It's a little like the rings of waves in a pool as drops of rain fall. The rings shift and change until, as more rain falls, they're so overlapped that they only exist for the instant the drop hits the pool. Then they're almost immediately something else entirely, affected by the waves formed by all the other drops.

This means that who we are is a function of who we're in relationship with. And, since we all breathe the same air and drink the same water[70] that means everybody on the planet, really – and could include everyone who's ever been on the planet and ever will be! Some people even remind us that we're all breathing atoms of the bodies of the Buddha, the Christ, Lincoln, and Hitler!

---

[70] John F. Kennedy used that phrase in his inaugural address. Daniel Nahmod used it in a song by the same name.

If that's how it is, how can we ever feel alone? How can we ever believe that we're isolated? How can we think that we can do anything that won't affect anyone else? Quite apart from the fact that everything we buy or throw away affects several other people!

Perhaps the most useful idea I learned in graduate school is the most fundamental principle of systems science: that the universe is one inter-connected whole, and that everything in it exists as part of that whole, in relationship with everything else. We can never do just one thing because we're connected to all aspects of the universe and they're all affected by our every action.

We are not isolated individuals.

We are part of what Unitarian-Universalists call "the interdependent web of existence", what Fritjof Capra described in his book, *The Web of Life*, constantly affecting and affected by all other beings on the planet.

In fact, we are fully integrated into a system of support that extends throughout, and according to some far beyond, the 3-dimensional universe and is designed for the fullest possible development of its members.

The inspirational medical doctor, Deepak Chopra, says in several places that our heart's desires are the seeds of our life's purpose, planted in our hearts before we were born. They are a part of us. Those deep desires, those fulfilling expressions of who we really are, are woven into the fabric of our being.

And, since we're a part of the larger whole – the fabric of who I am is woven into the fabric of my culture, my planet, and the universe – then the fulfillment of my heart's desire (and yours, too) is actually the fulfillment of the whole. How could it be otherwise?

Albert Einstein was very clear about this. In a letter he wrote in 1950, he said

A human being is a part of the whole, called by us "Universe," a part limited in time and space. He experiences himself, his thoughts and feelings as something separate from the rest – a kind of optical delusion of his consciousness. The striving to free oneself from this delusion is the one issue of true religion. Not to nourish it but to try to overcome it is the way to reach the attainable measure of peace of mind.[71]

Einstein has also been quoted by many as saying, "the most important question is whether or not the universe is a friendly place." And while I had no idea what that meant when I first heard it, I now have to admit that I agree: whether we believe we're in a scary world that requires us to fight and struggle for our existence, or whether we live by another set of beliefs – and supporting evidence – is the only important distinction.

What he and these other scholars found is that the universe, or Nature, or God, is both bountiful and friendly, and its laws and processes work to support our good, our development, our unfolding potential and capabilities.

All we have to do is to learn how to work in harmony with those processes and laws, rather than fight them – which is the point of all those translations of 19th-century writers that I did (called by some my "prosperity" books: *The New Science of Getting Rich, The New Master Key System, The New Game of Life,* and *Natural Abundance*). All of them teach us how to "get out of our own way" and *allow* the universe to grant us our heart's desires.

They all echo the wisdom of past ages:

> ➤ the Taoists, reminding us to do the least possible and flow with the "river" of the Tao;
> ➤ the Hebrew prophets, reminding us to focus "with a single eye" on the divine and be blessed;
> ➤ Jesus, telling us to ask that we may receive, that "according to thy faith" will it be unto us;
> ➤ the mystery schools, initiating us into the sacred awareness that our outer world and inner are one.

They're also echoed in the voices of modern teachers:

> ➤ Esther Hicks, speaking as "Abraham" in books, including *The Law of Attraction,* and in videos, especially *Chill*

---

[71] This and related quotes may be found on several sites on the internet, including Einstein-quotes.com, It was originally in a letter written in 1950, according to *The New York Times* (29 March 1972).

Out! tell us that everything we want is "downstream," so
stop working so hard to get upstream;

➢ Mike Dooley in *The Secret* and his own videos and website, informs us that "thoughts are things" and all we
have to do to have the things is to have the thoughts;

➢ Wayne Dyer, whose titles *You'll See it When You Believe it,*
Manifest Your Destiny, Change Your Thinking Change Your
Life, and *Wishes Fulfilled* say it all.

And many more.

So, truly, the universe is structured in such a way that our fulfillment is its goal – our fulfillment is a part of its fulfillment. Our
experiencing our heart's desires, achieving our potential, creating
what is ours to create, is how the universe is completed and fulfilled!

This means that of course we can "move mountains" and
heal and "get rich!" These are some of the things we were born to
be and do! It's just that in this world, this Empire culture of control and acquisition, we've been trained to forget how to do them.

Just what have we forgotten?

All the great spiritual teachers throughout human history
(which is the same as saying our Empire culture, the Mayans'
Long Count) have been trying to tell us that we can accomplish all
the things we can dream of by operating in harmony with, rather
than fighting, the harmonious flow of Universal principles and
processes.

When we do the kinds of processes outlined in Chapter 4 our
thoughts, feelings, intentions, and desires begin to be in alignment;
we feel the "flow." We begin to know we're in harmony with All
That Is; the Universe is our home, our body, our song.

Then experiences that can only be called miracles happen.

It's the goal of the 365 lessons and the text of *A Course in*
Miracles to get us to that place. In a spiraling series of deeper and
deeper experiences we're encouraged to:

➢ realize that nothing we see or sense is real – it's changeable, not eternal;

> ➤ accept that all people, together, are God's Son – any distinction is the result of a belief that separation is possible;
> ➤ let go of any idea of separation from God, and all the fear and anger that are associated with that idea;
> ➤ feel the life and love and freedom that comes with relaxing into the oneness with God that is Heaven on Earth;
> ➤ let go of any idea of separation or pain or anger or fear associated with other beings;
> ➤ feel, speak, and teach only the love between us.

It's the stated intention of the ancient Hindu guidelines, described in the several hundred Yoga Aphorisms of Patanjali, to get us to that place. They teach us to:

> ➤ learn to still the normal thought processes;
> ➤ feel the energy and wisdom of the universe flowing in and through the body;
> ➤ know that there is no separation between this self and the source of all being;
> ➤ learn to let go of competing desires;
> ➤ know that all needs are met and desires are fulfilled;
> ➤ allow a blissful state of being to become the norm, regardless of external circumstances.

It's the essence of the teachings of Jesus in the New Testament to get us to that place. Over and over, he tells us to:

> ➤ love everyone you meet as if there were no separation, no difference, no distinction between them and you;
> ➤ don't worry about others, possessions, or the future, relax and be joyful;
> ➤ ask knowing you have received, feeling that it's already done, giving thanks out of the sense that whatever you ask is already answered;
> ➤ see and experience the kingdom of Heaven that is at hand.

They're all saying that there truly is a way to experience Reality, the Kingdom of Heaven, *Samadhi*, the New World, here and now!

A friend of mine has made a commitment to live this new way and has developed a remarkable capacity for manifesting her desires and intentions. Actually, we all have this capacity, but she's more aware of it than most. As she and I have discussed and analyzed various "miraculous" events in her life over the past several years, we've found a number of consistencies. She's most effective when she's:

> ➢ playfully joyful and appreciative of life;
> ➢ not attached to a specific outcome, but open to possibilities in the direction of a feeling of satisfaction;
> ➢ able to let the idea go and focus on something else immediately.

So, for example, when someone has seemed to be seriously injured or ill, she's seen the most dramatic turnarounds when all three of these conditions were in place. A man walked away from an apparently deadly fall; a woman's "lumps" were not present at her next check-up; a tree fell in a totally unlikely direction.

Yet, whenever my friend became attached to a specific outcome or felt concern about the person, her results have been disappointing.

This is supported by the teachings of Emma Curtis Hopkins, as well as the teachings of Mary Baker Eddy's Christian Science.[72] Their student, Ernest Holmes, trained his Science of Mind practitioners to avoid thinking about the problem but to see and feel people as whole, well, and happy – now.[73] And Emmet Fox, author of the "second blue book" used in Alcoholics Anonymous, *The Sermon On The Mount*, describes a Golden Key: focus on the qualities of the divine rather than on the problem in front of you.

Contemplating this, I'm reminded that Jesus loved to party and often told his students (we call them disciples) to stop worrying. I also remember Psalm 98: "Sing a new song…" It's almost as

---

[72] *Science and Health with Key to the Scriptures* contains Eddy's guidelines for healing self and others.

[73] *Science of Mind* is Holmes' most complete set of guidelines.

if the universe, being a song, wants us to "sing a joyful song" to be in harmony, or resonance, with its processes.

Is that the new world that awaits us? A joyful song, no worries, and miraculous transformations on all sides?

The forecasts of the futurists offer some glimmers of hope for that kind of world, although the data needed for quantitative studies is hard to find on this subject.

The prophecies say that for some, over the next several decades, that is the direction the world is moving. They all say that while many will continue to choose the path of fear, greed, and discord, hanging on to stuff and people rather than developing in spirit, and so limiting their options, many more will experience the beauty, joy, peace, and harmony of the New World.

They say that those who feel lovingly connected with all life, who feel wealthy[74] and choose to live simply because they don't need more "stuff" to be happy, who work cooperatively with the laws of Nature and with each other, who share easily and feel a deep sense of gratitude – these people will experience a joyful shift into a new way of life. And that new life is one in which "miracles" are normal and synchronicities abound; in which the veil between dimensions is thin, and energy-bodies are easily perceived; in which the wisdom of the heart guides one through life, and the world is experienced as a safe and nurturing environment in which we're encouraged to create more and more delightful experiences and possibilities.

Love Makes the World Go 'Round

In the Judeo-Christian tradition, one of the names of God is Love. The founder of the Unity movement, Charles Fillmore, calls Love one of the twelve divine Powers of Man, represented by the disciple John, who was called "the beloved." The chorus of a 1970s Catholic hymn, quoting St. Paul, says

> *God is love*

---

[74] The word wealthy comes from the word *weal* meaning well-being.

and he who abides in love

abides in God

and God in him.

I often find that hymn floating around in the back of my mind as I
go through my day. (Nowadays, though, I'm a little more politically correct and say "we" instead of "he" and "us" instead of
"him.") It helps me remember that any sense of separation I
might experience is my own doing – my own thoughts and feelings of unworthiness or lack of love – and all I need to do is be
loving, to "abide in love," to know that I am loved and, in Truth,
am Love itself.

What's Love got to do with it?

When we were in graduate school, one of the more delightful
mental games I used to play with my kids' father (then husband,
now "wasband" and more like the brother I never had) was an
exploration of where gravity left off and love began. Is the attraction between us, the same as the attraction of any 2 units of
matter? Is it love or gravity or something else? And what would
that something else be? Does the moon love the earth? Does the
earth love the sun? Are we held on this planet because of mutual
love?

Now, when I consider that question, I add the Law of Attraction and the subatomic *boson*, which is best defined not as a thing
but as a tendency to come together. At the most basic level, all
matter and energy exists because of this subatomic tendency to
come together. The logical extension is that all "coming together"
in the universe is a function of the intensity of this tendency,
whether it looks like gravity or magnetism or human beings attracting each other or whatever we're focusing on. So, in terms of
what they accomplish, love and gravity *could well be* the same thing!

We might say then, that everything that has a form is a result
of the fundamental tendency to come together, or Love. Our
planet is rocks that formed from stardust coming together; our
sun is quantum particles coming together; our rivers and oceans
are molecules of water coming together; our bodies are chemicals

coming together as cells and organs and working together as systems.

This means that, in a loosely defined way, everything has form because the tendency to come together, which is a definition of Love, exists. We can even say that all our interactions with other beings are Love – they are a function of the tendency to come together.

Not too surprisingly, this is one of the messages of *A Course in Miracles*. In various ways and places it says that all of our interactions are expressions of Love or requests for Love – even though they may not always look like it – and when we realize that, we are free.

That was a hard one for me to get. I had experienced some physical abuse growing up and I wasn't comfortable with the idea that those actions could be called Love. Then I remembered that, after it was over, there would almost always be tears and the rare statement that "I love you!" Later, when I had my own children, I realized that every painful childhood incident I remembered could be translated as "I love you and want you to love me in a way I can recognize it!" That was when I could have compassion for the person, who after all had been abused while growing up. Then I could get over my anger, pain, frustration, and tendency to act out the same behaviors (though certainly not condoning the action!). I'm grateful to say that it was a proud moment when I realized my youngest was 18 and I hadn't continued the pattern – and it's even more wonderful to watch my eldest parenting her young ones with enduring patience and understanding!

Say You Love Me...

Remember a few chapters back, about the power of our words? Whatever we say – or rather, whatever we think and feel while we're saying something – has the power to change our experience. When what we say and what we feel and what we imagine are all in alignment, all supporting each other without any conflict, then our word is pure power: we can, as Jesus promised "move mountains… heal the sick … raise the dead." Thousands of Science of Mind and Christian Science practitioners, and as many

Charismatic Christian faith healers, have proven this to be so, and modern consciousness research is supporting their results.

"I love you," as most men in our culture know, is not something to be said lightly. However, *not* saying it causes more pain and shuts down more lives than most of us can imagine. When we don't say it and mean it, we don't open that part of us that can receive the Love that is inherent in the universe, the unconditional Love that we call God. And when that doesn't happen, a part of us dies.

Many of us have had to learn this the hard way. Too often, it's taken a scary diagnosis or catastrophic event for us to stop and discover how to begin.

In my own life, it took having children. When I learned to say "I love you" to my children in a way that was fully aligned (which I had to learn, not having experienced it in a healthy way growing up), they got it. And, as I did so, I could feel not only my own feelings of appreciation, delight, joy, and longing for their wellbeing, I could also feel something opening up in me and in them at that moment, something by which whatever feelings we had for each other were enhanced, increased, enriched. Later I realized that in that moment I began to feel the power of Love that we call God.

When that happened, I began to understand the nature of unconditional love. I began to realize that it didn't matter if we had been angry just a minute before, or if any of us did something one of us didn't like, the love between us would remain. It was permanent, eternal.

That realization carried me through the process when, years later, it became clear that their father and I no longer had a marriage. As I allowed myself to experience and release the issues that had accumulated over our relationship, I kept coming back to the love that had brought us together. So I made a claim for our future: "regardless of the form of our relationship, the love we share will continue." I held on to that thought through the long process of dividing up our household and ferrying our children between two states. And, happily, over a decade later, we continue to be loving with each other.

Love, I came to understand, is a verb. It's not a feeling that comes and goes, but a decision and set of actions. And it doesn't depend on the form of relationship we have with the other person. As Emma Curtis Hopkins says in her first lesson, "Love is not something that comes to us in any one person; that is but a sign of the ongoing presence of the eternal Love that we call God."[75] So "I love you" is, ideally, something that we can say – and feel – to all people, all beings, since they're all the embodiment of the intelligent matter-energy we call God.

How can I love everyone? How could anyone?

The English language has its limitations, and this is one of them. Just as the Arctic peoples have many different words for the different forms of what we call "snow," other cultures have different words for the different forms of what we call love.

In ancient Greek, the language that the New Testament letters were written in, the word that is translated into English as "love" might be either *agape* or *philia,* or even *pragma.* Only the lusty attraction of romantic love is called *eros.*

In his first letter to the Corinthian church, the apostle Paul tells his congregation that *agape* is the greatest of qualities they can have: meaning a generalized love for each other and the whole creation; it's also the word the Greeks used to translate the Hebrew commandment to "Love God with all you soul and mind, and your neighbor as your self.". In Paul's letter to the Roman church he tells them to "Love one another with a brotherly affection," encouraging *philia* (which is also the root of the city name: Philadelphia). In Greek, the kind of love that develops over a long, committed relationship is called *pragma.* In Greek, *phlautia* is the idea of self-care or self-love, which is something we're all learning to do in this age of CoViD. Then there is how we love the people in our families, that deep affection and unconditional acceptance of one another that the Greeks called *storje.*

---

[75] In Lesson One of her various texts, including my interpretation: *Unveiling Your Hidden Power.*

What if you're in a committed relationship?

For most of us, to say those words in a way that's fully aligned, in a way that our heart and soul and mind all agree, we need to be able to look at someone or think about them and experience a deep connection, a deep recognition of something in them that pulls us into that alignment. And, in our culture, that kind of connection is reserved for our lover, our spouse, our parents, our children, and our best friend. We can't look at just anyone and say such things without social consequences.

The upside of a committed, personal relationship is that it's like a crucible for all our issues. The people we feel that way about are most able to help us bring our past issues to the surface where they can be worked on, and are the most supportive of the process as we go through it – unless we're bringing up their issues, of course; then things may not seem very loving for a while.

The downside is that we may fall into the trap that *A Course in Miracles* calls a "special relationship," in which we think that love only comes in certain forms with certain people under certain conditions.

This suggests that the need for people in committed personal relationships will be to mature into what the *Course* calls a "Holy Relationship," in which our love for the individual becomes an expression of our love for All-That-Is – what the Greeks called *agape*.

This is why the spiritual teachers of all traditions have said that if someone needs that kind of connection to feel that kind of love, they're best off not trying to live without it. From Lao T'se to Jesus to Mohammed to the Dalai Lama and virtually every abbot and mother superior in every monastic tradition, they say that the monastic, celibate life is for people who can "fall in love" with everyone and everything, rather than focusing on just one person. Like the Mother Superior in *The Sound of Music,* they tell those of us who need to focus on one person to use the practice of loving that one person *fully* as our way to come closer to God's eternal, universal, unconditional Love. The same applies to our families. In the Hindu tradition that path is called *Bakhti Yoga*.

Living in Love

Either way, in love with one person and our family members, or with the All-That-Is, we get to practice saying "I love you" in a way that is fully aligned, and to feel that opening of our being to something greater than us. We get to decide and re-decide, commit and re-commit, to act in loving ways. We get to *be* the unconditional love that is our birthright as part of this intelligent matter-energy system we call the Universe.

And as we do so, we begin to experience more and more of what may only be called miracles:

> ➤ The world that was built up from the fear that grew out of our belief that we were isolated and alone begins to dissolve.

> ➤ A new world, "a new heaven and a new earth," begins to take its place.

> ➤ The sun shines more brightly, and the darkness is a welcome "empty fullness" out of which wonderful things are created.

> ➤ There's a growing sense of wonder and delight; the cycles of highs and lows are less intense and more consistently high.

> ➤ The people around us are more supportive and understanding; they listen better, and we do, too.

> ➤ Amazing new possibilities emerge from our interactions, in true dialogue (a Greek word that means "through the word," beautifully described in David Bohm's book, *On Dialogue*).

> ➤ The things we do come more easily and the things we don't do bring our dreams to life more directly. Synchronicities abound.

Is Such a World Possible?

Indeed! All indicators say that the old world *is* passing away, now. Our hearts and souls have long known it and our minds are beginning to understand it. The Love that we are is overcoming the fear that we were taught to believe in. Nature is no longer our adversary but is, more and more, our guiding friend and nurturing supporter. Everyone we meet is more loving and loveable. And, we discover, all of us are increasingly whole and healthy and more and more fulfilled in our daily activities and interactions.

This is the promise of the new era and the new culture emerging in it. And this is what the data is beginning to show us. (If you want graphs check out my website sharings page: http://ruthlmillerphd.com/sharings/whats-the-world-coming-to).

This is why so many people desperately want the world we've been struggling in for so many years to go away, to make room for this new world, which is so alive in our hearts, to become our experience. That is why, even when we don't know it, we act in ways that will bring that ending about.

And that is why, when we allow ourselves to really know what we think and feel, we look at everything going to pieces around us and think, "Hooray! At last! The World is ending!" And then we feel the dream of the emerging new world, based on love and cooperation, discovery and sharing, balance and harmony with Nature and our spirit, begin to show up in our hearts and in our surroundings.

And so it is.

In Appreciation

Make the World Go Away
(by Hank Cochran, ©1963)

Chorus:

Make the world go away

And get it off my shoulders.

Say the things you used to say

And make the world go away.

2nd verse:

I'm sorry if I hurt you;

I'll make it up to you some day;

Just say you love me like you used to

And make the world go away.

This book began to write itself in early August, 2010, shaped by the words above. It was some months later that we discovered that Hank had passed on in July. Recognizing this synchronicity and Hank's generosity of spirit, we dedicate these pages to his memory - and to the children who will live in the world we are creating today.

Index

About the Author

Ruth-Ellen L Miller, Ph.D. *integrates scientific, spiritual, and cultural understanding to clarify metaphysical principles and practices in a way that the "rest of us" can understand them.*

With degrees in anthropology, cybernetics, environmental studies, and the systems sciences, she was a college professor and futurist before being training and ordained as a New Thought minister, serving Unitarian, Unity, and Science of Mind churches in the Pacific Northwest. She is now also Director of Research for Gaia Living Systems Institute.

Her Library of Hidden Knowledge books (Beyond Words/ Simon & Schuster) include: Natural Abundance, Ralph Waldo Emerson's Guidelines for Prosperity, The New Science of Getting Rich, As We Think-So We Are, The New Master Key System *and more. Her Paths of Power biographies introduce New Thought leaders; her guidelines for spiritual practice include* Uncommon Prayer, Spiritual Success, Unveiling Your Hidden Power, *and* Coming into Freedom *(WiseWoman Press).*

She has also written about how healing happens. Calm Healing *co-authored with Robert Bruce Newman, is an explanation of meditation as a healing modality, (North Atlantic Books). And her original history of New Thought healing,* 150 Years of Healing, *has been updated as* The Science of Mental Healing *(Portal Center Press).*

Mary's Power: embracing the divine feminine as the age of empire and invasion ends *(Portal Center Press) explores women's role and abilities in our spiritual history and understanding.*

Ruth's website is www.ruthlmillerphd.com

Other Titles from Portal Center Press

Awakening, a journey of enlightenment,
by Andree Cuenod

Butterfly Soup, changing your life from the inside out
by Aurora J. Miller

Kat's 9 Lives, moving passion into action for a "feel good" life,
by Kat Cunningham

*Mary's Power, embracing the Divine Feminine as the age of empire
ends,* by Ruth L Miller

Miracles through Music, the odyssey of a Healer
by Joel Andrews

To Restore Earth's Balance: Awakening an Already Knowing
by Milt Markewitz & Ruth L Miller

*Views from the Pew, moving beyond religion: discovering truth
within,* by J C Pedigo and friends

Wake UP! Our Old Beliefs Don't Work Anymore!
by Andree Cuenod

**Portal
Center
Press**

www.portalcenterpress.com

www.ingramcontent.com/pod-product-compliance
Lightning Source LLC
Chambersburg PA
CBHW071213020426
42333CB00015B/1393